I'LL
GIVE IT
TO YOU
STRAIGHT
-ish

I'LL GIVE IT TO YOU STRAIGHTISH

What Your Teen Wants You to Know

MAX DUBROW

WITH DR. JUDY HO

FLASH POINT

To my fellow teens who have felt alone and lost in this complicated world: I truly hope you find solace, and that my shared experiences help your parents support you with compassion and understanding. And to my amazing family, who have been there for me every step of the way.

Published by Flashpoint™ Books, Seattle
www.flashpointbooks.com

Produced by Girl Friday Productions
www.girlfridayproductions.com

Design: Rachel Marek
Development & editorial: Katherine Richards
Production editorial: Jaye Whitney Debber

Cover photography by Greg Loza

All images courtesy of the author except:
Cover, 2, 5 (portrait), © Greg Loza; Cover and throughout
(paper rip), 32 pixels/SS; 20, 70, 116 (paint), tofutyklein/SS;
20, 140 (phone), Olha Polishchuk/SS; 46 (paper), Flas100/SS;
92 (sparkle), Efetova Anna/SS; 92 (frame), Fosin/SS; 92 (tape),
Yevgenij_D/SS; 140 (glitter), aDrew/SS *(SS: Shutterstock)*

ISBN (paperback): 978-1-954854-30-7
ISBN (e-book): 978-1-954854-23-9

Library of Congress Control Number: 2021916288

First edition

CONTENTS

FOREWORD

A s a parent, I always seek out resources to help my kids, but sometimes they are the best resource of all. Max has insights well beyond her years, and I learned so much by reading this book. I wish I'd had a guide like this when she was younger. I could have avoided a lot of rookie parenting mistakes.

In this book, Max takes us on a journey of what it actually feels like to be a teenager today. She talks about how teens are trying to navigate life and what they need us to know. Dr. Judy Ho does an amazing job of adding her expertise to help us fully understand the workings of the modern teenage mind.

The way we grew up is vastly different than what our kids are going through, and that's essential to understand. In addition to all of the normal growing pains we experienced as teens, today's kids have social media, the internet, instant access to almost anything, and an impossible bar to reach to access a four-year college. As I've seen firsthand with my children, even with good, solid parents, counselors, and friends, the task of getting through this period of time can be isolating and daunting. Finding ways to communicate with your kids is key. Parents typically want to talk at their kids—teach them and impart their wisdom—when what they should be doing is listening.

As a mother with four kids, I want to say thank-you to Max for writing such an open, honest, raw (and sometimes uncomfortable) account of your experiences with life, anxiety, sexuality, and beyond. You will help so many people by sharing these thoughts and stories.

—HEATHER DUBROW

(Oh, and, Max, if you are reading this . . . as *your* mother, I want to say I am immensely proud of you for taking a dark time in your life and using it to help others. I love you.)

by Max

Hi! I'm Max Dubrow. I am so excited you are here to read this book. Well, I'm excited . . . *and* I'm also a little nervous. Nervous because in the pages ahead, I share a lot about my personal experiences and what they've taught me (and what I hope they might be able to teach others). Don't get me wrong—this is definitely not a teen tell-all full of melodrama and gossip; it's more like a teen tell-*some*, with the "some" being shared to help illuminate the lessons I've learned as a young person navigating the modern world.

I would have never thought of myself as a person who would be sharing much of anything with an audience in this way. I've struggled with anxiety, including social anxiety, since I was eleven. So putting myself out there is one of the things that makes me want to just curl up in my bed all day.

The truth is that I've had to be somewhat "out there" for a while, though. My parents have starred in the reality TV shows *The Real Housewives of Orange County* and *Botched* since I was nine and eleven, respectively. While I don't remember most of it, and I never really had to be involved in much of the TV and filming stuff, I do remember growing up with our lives not being entirely private. And I remember being part of the social media community—and having a presence there—from a young age.

Still, I was most comfortable kind of leading my somewhat low-key life. But something happened in the last few years that changed that and made me want to put my own voice out into the world: I came out as bisexual. I had so many teens reach out, thanking me for being open about my sexuality, that it made me realize how little teen queer representation there was. I decided that I could use my platform to help broaden this representation, and in August of 2020, I started my podcast called *I'll Give It to You Straightish*.

THE START OF *STRAIGHTISH*

When I first started *I'll Give It to You Straightish*, I knew I was going to talk about my experiences as a teen in Gen Z. I hoped in doing so, I would help make teens who were having experiences similar to mine feel less alone and maybe even discover a different approach to working through or solving their problems. On the podcast so far, I've covered topics such as sexuality, plastic surgery, and mental health. It's been so rewarding, but it's also been challenging to share my experiences. Not only because these are so personal to me but also because sometimes I've felt like I don't know enough to be giving advice on how to manage the teenage years. I'm still a teen, living and learning my way through it. But what I've realized is that I can share what's worked for me and the insights I've gained from my parents or other adults, and people can take and leave what they want.

One thing I didn't expect, however, was the fact that a lot of parents started listening to what I had to say on the podcast. They wanted to learn and hear what it's like from the teen perspective, and let's face it, if they're parents of teens or soon-to-be teens, they may not be hearing much from their own children. (If you're reading this, fellow teens, I really am on your side; I won't give away all our secrets, but I will try to share enough to help your parents better understand the challenges we face today and how they can best support you.)

Because of the outpouring of love and support from many parents and teens across the country about my podcast, I decided to write a book. It seems like the issues teens are facing only continue to grow—hello, global pandemic and an increasing takeover of technology, not to mention worries about climate change and greater awareness and activism around racism. And these feel unique to today's teen generation—no adult had to face the same mix of issues when they were our age. It's more important now than ever to offer an insider perspective that may lead parents to discover a new approach to helping their kids through changes and challenges.

Just like with my podcast, I've pulled the topics that I'll discuss in this book from my personal experiences, but I know these are also common areas that are challenging for all teens—and usually their parents too. I decided to focus on six general topics: anxiety, social media, school and other pressures, friendships, dating and relationships, and sexuality. It's not like I've figured these things all out 100 percent; in fact, I'm still struggling with or working through many issues in these areas. This is why I'm so excited that the amazing Dr. Judy Ho has added her clinical perspective and guidance throughout the book. Dr. Judy is a board-certified clinical and forensic neuropsychologist and a tenured professor at Pepperdine University. She works with patients of all ages with complex mental health concerns, including youth depression, anxiety, and substance abuse issues. She offers some amazing insights in the book, so be sure to watch for her additions throughout in the sections called "Dr. Judy's Notes."

I know there are other topics besides the six that we chose that I could have tried to explore and write about, but I really wanted to stay focused on what I could filter directly through my own experiences. And while my life is different, and yeah, I come from a family with money and some fame, I still struggle with crippling anxiety, the stress of trying to prepare for a super-tough test, the heartache of someone not liking me back . . . and these are things that so many people can relate to. I am lucky in so many ways, but I'm also just another human being trying to make it through this life while staying happy and healthy.

The truth is, I wish my parents had had access to a book like this when I was a young teen or a middle schooler; it might have helped them better understand what I was going through. So I hope that my shared experiences will land in the hands of someone who can use them, whether it's a parent who gains enough insight on their kid's perspective that they increase their compassion and feel more confident in giving advice or a teen who benefits from parents who can better guide them through challenges with school, mental health, dating, sexuality, and more.

I hope you enjoy and get something out of *I'll Give It to You Straightish*!

Max Dubrow

SHE/HER

by Dr. Judy Ho

Parents, let's be honest. Have you ever secretly rolled your eyes or sighed in exasperation when your teen tells you that you don't understand them and what they're going through or complains about how stressed out they are? When they make a mountain out of a molehill or become agitated in seemingly innocuous situations, do you think they're being just a tad dramatic? As they get more irritable at your questions or when they tell you they just want to be left alone, do you ever think to yourself, "Do you know how easy you have it?" or "If you only knew what it's like to be an adult with *real* problems and responsibilities?"

If any of the above sounds like you, you're not alone. It's perfectly normal for parents to have these reactions when they see their teens struggle and complain about what's going on in their lives. Although

I'm sure you try your best to be as compassionate and helpful as you can most of the time, there are also those moments where you can lose your patience with them because you really just don't see things the way they do or you think maybe they're blowing things out of proportion—just a little. Add that to the pressures of your own stress and problems that you also need to manage, and it can sometimes feel increasingly difficult to relate to your teen and help them thrive without losing your own mind!

If you think your life is stressful, here's something that might surprise you. According to a survey conducted by the American Psychological Association, American teens say that they experience stress levels similar to those of adults, especially during the school year—when they report even higher stress than adults. Teens stated that their school-year stress levels far exceeded what they believe to be healthy, and even more concerning, teens seem to underestimate the impact that stress can have on their mental and physical well-being. According to the National Institutes of Health, nearly one in three teens between the ages of thirteen and eighteen will experience an anxiety disorder, with numbers climbing in recent years. Seventy percent of teens say anxiety and depression are major problems among their peers, with an additional 26 percent saying they are minor problems. Depression has also become increasingly common among US teens, with 13 percent of American teens describing at least one major depressive episode in the past year (up from 8 percent a decade ago). The rates of depression are especially alarming among teen girls, who are almost three times as likely as teen boys to have experienced depression. Even more concerning is the rise in the numbers of youth admitted to children's hospitals for thoughts of suicide or self-harm— with rates more than double those from ten years ago.

As we adults go through our daily lives, which are full of pressure and responsibilities, we may not always be completely in tune with some of the lesser-known yet very real pressures that our teens are facing. Myriad factors—biological, emotional, social, and psychological— constantly affect our twenty-first-century teens and make their existence extremely complicated. Your teen's personality, repertoire of coping strategies, and unique life experiences, in addition to the stressors specific to this place and time in history, also play a role in creating pressures that they may not have the tools to deal with effectively. Here are just a few issues that most of today's teens will experience at some point during their development:

INCREASING SOCIAL PRESSURES COMPOUNDED BY THE PREVALENCE OF SOCIAL MEDIA

Something that we parents didn't have to go through in quite the same way is the ever-present influence of social media and digital means of communication. More and more, we see that teens are basing their self-esteem and well-being on what happens online—who likes their posts, how many followers they have, and what other people are posting about—and comparing their lives to others' highlight reels. This makes it hard to achieve a positive self-concept that is secure and stable, because every day can bring about something new in the world of social media that they didn't expect.

HIDDEN AND NOT-SO-HIDDEN BULLYING, OFTEN WITH AN INSIDIOUS ONLINE COMPONENT

Bullying can be very traumatic for children, and you may even remember your own experiences of being bullied as a child. But something that we didn't have to deal with is online bullying. It has become increasingly easy to say mean and hurtful things while hiding behind a screen, and whether your teen knows the person who is bullying them or not (perpetrators of cyberbullying can be unknown people from all over the world), the impact on their psyche is just as negative as that of in-person bullying—or perhaps worse. Online bullying can be even more incessant than in-person bullying because it doesn't require the bully to be in the same place as your teen. In a matter of minutes, the bully can hurl dozens of insults and derogatory comments, all without any real consequences.

FRIGHTENING AND THREATENING REAL-LIFE EVENTS THAT SEEM TO BE MORE PERVASIVE THAN IN YEARS PAST

School shootings, sadly, have been on the rise, along with other scary events like natural disasters and various forms of unrest in our country and around the world, and because of increasing media coverage over a number of platforms that did not exist when we were kids (like social media, online news programs, streaming TV, and far more channels on cable than we can possibly consume), we hear more about it and for longer periods of time. At the writing of this book, we are still struggling with the COVID-19 pandemic, which has caused fear, anxiety, and stress for everyone and resulted in severe limitations on our usual ways of relating to others, exploring hobbies, and engaging in learning opportunities. This has been a lengthy period of immense stress that will have ramifications for how we socialize and engage with one another for years to come. In addition, the current political climate is extremely divisive, with no clear end in sight, not to mention concerns about racism and related tensions, intersectional inequities, the state of world affairs, and the climate crisis; these conversations are increasingly making their way into the regular discussions that older teens have as well. And as teens search for answers to all of society's problems, they may stumble onto wild conspiracy theories that leave their minds spinning and make it even harder for them to cope.

HIGH EXPECTATIONS AND PRESSURE TO SUCCEED

This is likely relatable to many of you who were high achievers yourselves—but today's teens experience a culture of achievement that may be even more intense than what you experienced. A report by the Robert Wood Johnson Foundation listed "excessive pressure to excel" as one of the top conditions harming adolescent wellness. People are talking about teen achievement more and more in regular conversations among family members and in the online spotlight of social media, and a college degree is becoming the minimum requirement for many entry-level jobs. Today's teens are pressured to take the hardest classes, get into the most exclusive universities, and obtain as much extracurricular and volunteer experience as possible in order to stand out on college applications. Periodic economic downturns, job automation, and globalization in a very competitive job market create job and career uncertainty as teens approach adulthood. This all adds up to anxiety growing to an even bigger problem by the time they are in college, with nearly two-thirds of college students reporting overwhelming anxiety, up from 50 percent five years earlier, with common symptoms including feelings of dread, panic attacks, fatigue, headaches, and stomachaches.

SEARCHING FOR THEIR UNIQUE IDENTITY WHILE TRYING TO FIT IN

The teen years are a crucial time when youth discover who they are, what they're made of, their likes and dislikes, and their longer-term goals. And it can be really hard to balance wanting to stand out with also wanting to fit in with others. In particular, teens may grapple with how to feel accepted, cherished, and valued by others while not acting too needy or like they don't have a mind of their own. Peer stress is a pervasive problem, and research shows that it can negatively affect academic performance and well-being.

FEELING OUT OF CONTROL OF THEIR OWN LIVES

As adults, we can generally make decisions for ourselves. But that's not the case for teens. They have to answer to parents, other family members, teachers, tutors, coaches, and other important adults—many of whom may have conflicting agendas or plans for the teen (even if the adults are acting from a place of wanting to be helpful). There are only twenty-four hours in a day, and teens may have very different ideas of how they want to spend that time compared with what their parents, teachers, and coaches want. And when teens assert themselves (even for good reason), they are sometimes shut down by adults because these acts can be viewed as rebellion or disobedience. A sense of control over your life is associated with self-confidence and well-being, so feeling that lack of control can be a huge risk factor for experiencing chronic stress, lowered self-esteem, and clinical problems like depression and anxiety. (Not to mention that the COVID-19 pandemic may have exacerbated feelings of loss of control for teens and adults alike.)

These are just a handful of the types of problems unique to our teenagers today that cause them to feel pressured and overwhelmed. I know this feels like a lot to take in, but the great news is that we can do a lot to help our teens to cope with these problems too. As a board-certified clinical and forensic neuropsychologist with a developed specialty in youth mental health, I was so excited when Max approached me to help with this book. I know Max really wants to offer insight and understanding that can both help teens to thrive and also help parents to provide better support for their children. With the practical advice and evidence-based tips you'll encounter in this book, you'll gain the confidence to help your teen excel during these challenging years while staying calm yourself. This book will be a valuable resource for you to navigate some of the most common difficulties today's teens experience. Know that whatever challenges you're facing today, you're not alone. Max and I are here for you, and we want to help you to do your very best in creating a bright, fulfilling, and meaningful today and future for your teen.

Clinical and forensic neuropsychologist, tenured professor, and author of *Stop Self-Sabotage*

I'LL
GIVE IT
TO YOU
STRAIGHT
-ish

CHAPTER 1

UNDER PRESSURE

How Heavy It All Feels . . .

I t's not easy being a kid these days. Parents expect a lot from their children, especially between the ages of ten and eighteen. Most of these expectations are school related, but there's also a lot of pressure to figure out what you want to do with your life and to know how to handle *all* situations, including family-related issues and mental health challenges.

The pressure starts early in life. If you want to get into a good college, it feels like you have to start preparing for your applications when you're four. If you want to do anything competitively, whether it's in sports or the arts, you need to have already dedicated so much effort to those activities by the time you reach double digits.

I realize that parents don't always have control over these issues and that they're just responding to the way things are today and trying to help their kids (or they think that's what they're doing). But if you're a kid, it's really over-whelming to try to keep up—and sometimes parents and adults dis-miss anything you might say about this. If you say it seems like school or life feels overwhelming, their response is—at least at first—to think you're whining or not tough enough or that your life is definitely not as hard as theirs was. I think there's a better way to respond to the challenges faced by kids today, and it starts with listening.

THE WEIGHT OF UNENDING ACADEMIC EXPECTATIONS

By far, the number-one pressure in many kids' lives is school pressure, and this pressure comes from every direction . . . parents, teachers, peers, et cetera. When a parent asks the question, "How's school?" and most kids just say, "Fine," "Good," or "Whatever," they're probably actually thinking things like the following.

"THERE'S WAY TOO MUCH WORK BEING ASSIGNED."

I was in third grade when I really started to be stressed out by the amount of work we were being assigned. I distinctly remember that third grade was hard. There was so much planning and so many projects that we had to use an agenda. It felt like a lot as an eight-year-old.

Then, in middle school, I remember having hours of homework each night, which I was supposed to finish and turn in for excellent grades and still have a life that included theater or other after-school activities. And I had to make sure to spend time with my family, try to maintain friendships in some way, and do extracurriculars that would make me stand out to high schools.

Of course, it only gets worse in high school. At that time, you're supposed to do all your homework, which, if you're taking any AP classes, is an extreme amount of work; finish all your ongoing projects; do your community service; be an athlete (if you play sports); be in

> *"I wish my parents knew that school is way different than it was twenty or thirty years ago. Tests are a lot harder, and standards are up."*
>
> —B., Washington, sixteen

clubs; and try to keep up those same family and friend relationships. It's just so unrealistic, and what ends up happening is that when trying to do everything, we end up procrastinating or trying to prioritize, maybe unsuccessfully, but then it becomes even *more* stressful.

What also gets piled on top of all this is the fact that a lot of teachers seem to forget that we have six other classes, or whatever it might be, and expect us to be able to fully focus on just their one class, but that's impossible. Some teachers are resistant to hearing a student say that they don't understand how something was explained or how an assignment is supposed to work. These teachers will suggest that it's the student's fault for not studying the information, but that's not always the case. Teachers have different styles of teaching, and sometimes it's not easy to immediately get a teacher's style.

Even when there are multiple factors to consider, it seems like parents default to saying their child is procrastinating or being lazy if they don't do well in school. Maybe this is because a parent doesn't want to blame the school or teachers for giving too much work because they have a fear that it will signal that their kid is just not capable of keeping up. But this lack of listening is precisely why some kids will shut down when the topic of school comes up. They'll talk about it with their friends, like I do with mine, because sometimes it feels like it's only your classmates who understand.

"THE 'POSITIVE' ENCOURAGEMENT IS NOT SO POSITIVE."

When I was in third grade, I remember they had this method of grouping students after each year/class. Depending on your performance in some area, you would either end up in the "Hall of Fame" or the "Hall of Shame." Can you imagine being eight years old and going to the Hall of Shame because you didn't get all your homework in? Talk about making you feel bad about yourself when you're just a young kid. I remember being stressed about this.

In middle school, a similar practice ensued. They would have a ceremony twice a year where the faculty would group the student body together and give out awards. The kids with straight As would get blue certificates. Once they handed these out, the kids who got one B would receive a red certificate. Any other kids would get no awards, which was made clear to the entire student body.

"MY CHILDHOOD SEEMS TO HAVE DISAPPEARED."

As a young kid, you might not notice the shift from being a full-on kid to a kid who's starting to experience stress about school. It's only later that you can look back and see it. For me, I can look back now and see that school stress began in third grade, when I started to experience the seeds of anxiety.

But it really built up by middle school, for me and for a lot of my classmates. I know a lot of people from middle school who never went out and never got to do anything because they had so much schoolwork to do.

Where I go to school, middle school means sixth grade through eighth grade . . . so about ages twelve to fifteen. I know it's different in other places, where middle school might start at fifth grade or go through ninth grade. It's sad to think of kids that age not being able to do fun stuff because it's kind of like the end of childhood. I know a lot of people who became so absorbed in school and grades around this time that they matured really fast and seemed to shift out of that kid space where things were fun and carefree.

What's absurd is that middle school isn't really getting you anywhere . . . or at least where I live, most high schools don't have that selective of a process. So it's like you're just working your butt off for parent approval, I guess. Meanwhile, you have no time to find yourself or your interests or anything because you're so busy with school and sticking to the curriculum.

AN INTENSE WORKLOAD AT A YOUNG AGE CAN CHANGE A KID, AND IT'S WORTH LISTENING TO YOUR PRETEEN OR TEEN IF THEY SAY THEY FEEL OVERWORKED.

It makes more sense not to get to have a life in high school because at least you are working toward a goal that you've kind of created for yourself. At least by that point, you know if you want to work hard to get into college or whatever your goal might be.

In either case, once that shift occurs, it can start to feel like you're working toward the next goal your entire life. You're never in the present moment because you're looking toward your grades, and then how those grades affect high school, and how those grades apply toward college, and then how you're going to get into the best colleges and go to the best states or whatever it might be. And with that, your childhood is over. It happens really fast, so fast you don't even realize it.

I guess what I'm trying to say is that an intense workload at a young age can change a kid, and it's worth listening to your preteen or teen if they say they feel overworked. And if you are the kid, speak up! No one knows what you're going through until you communicate it.

"ONCE I GOT GOOD/GREAT GRADES, YOU EXPECTED ME TO GET THEM FOREVER."

I started getting good grades when I was young, which I'm proud of, but it's also something that kind of haunted me because my parents just expected it—and still expect it—of me always.

I'll compare this with the case of my brother, who hasn't always gotten the best grades. When he gets good grades, he gets praised excessively, whereas if I get just good grades—not great—I get questioned about my performance. Even if this is indicative of our school priorities, I still think my parents should keep that same energy for both of us. It's kind of a bad cycle because it almost makes you not want to do well so that you don't have to constantly live up to those expectations.

Of course, I would never do that because I'm obsessed with my grades, but if my grades change, I would like the chance for it to be seen as maybe not entirely my fault. If my typical performance is to get As, and one semester I get all Bs, maybe something else is going on. Maybe it was a really difficult teacher, or the class was significantly harder, or maybe I was having a bad mental health year. There are other factors to be considered that parents often overlook or invalidate.

"MY MENTAL HEALTH ISSUES DON'T JUST SHUT OFF MAGICALLY WHEN IT'S TIME FOR SCHOOL."

I think expecting your child to get perfect grades all the time is unfair, especially because it's so hard on kids' mental well-being. What I also think is strange is when parents are super supportive regarding mental health issues and their kids—say, if they have anxiety or depression—but then they don't apply that support when it comes to school. I don't think they really realize that not only is school a contributing factor, but it's also not possible to just "turn off" anxiety or depression when it's time for class or time to do homework.

Of course, if you're a parent and you're not supportive regarding your kid's mental health issues, I hope you'll reconsider—although I think sometimes parents just don't know what to do or how to help. Fortunately, there are many options for mental health support. For

TEEN TALK

"Getting straight As doesn't mean we are mentally healthy."
—E., Pennsylvania, sixteen

example, a school nurse might be able to provide a referral, and there are also community-based federally and state-funded mental health services that anyone can access. See the Resources section at the end of the book for more options.

THE PROMISE OF FUN AFTER HIGH SCHOOL

My parents always say to me, "You will have fun after high school." Like, "Have your fun, but focus on your grades, and the fun will come later." Which is great, and I get that college will be fun, but at this point, I feel like I've been stressed for years, waiting to get to this la-la land of college so that I can take a break. But we all know college is not going to be a break at all; it's just higher-level learning—and higher-cost learning—with increased levels of stress.

Let me be clear that I want to go to college; I can't wait to go to college, and I'm going to do everything that I need to do to get into the best school possible. These days that means doing a lot of community service, completing an internship, participating in at least a dozen different clubs, spending time on college planning, taking college essay workshops, taking a yearlong class to study for the ACT, taking and retaking the ACT, taking early college classes, and doing as many other extracurriculars as I can squeeze into my already-packed days and nights. I'm doing these things because, like every other kid I know, I've been told by a college counselor, "These are the things you have to do to get into college."

There's so much competition that it leads to tension with your classmates at your own school. Talking about grades and test scores is just asking to start a fight. Everyone's vying for these seemingly few spots, and this is the feeling students have at their own schools—never mind the fact that there are kids across the country and globe also competing for the same spots! Even if you want to support your friends, there's a lot of comparing that starts to happen, as well as questioning of your

DR. JUDY'S NOTES

PREVENTING FAILURE-TO-LAUNCH SYNDROME AND HELPING TEENS DEVELOP HEALTHY INDEPENDENCE

The teen years are a crucial time for self-development. This is when teens consider who they are, solidify their self-concept, work on their self-esteem, and test the waters as they inch closer and closer to adulthood. And sometimes, it can be difficult to know how to balance independence with *inter*dependence, which is the healthy reliance on a supportive circle of people in order to keep learning and growing.

I work with many parents who, out of the goodness of their hearts and love for their children, end up coddling them and trying to protect them from every possible problem that could happen. Not only is this an impossible task, but in excessive doses, it can lead to failure-to-launch syndrome, which occurs in older teens or young adults who struggle with developmental transitions into early adulthood. This can happen when parents don't give children the opportunity to face age-appropriate challenges that allow them to develop skills and confidence. The result is that they may have

> **SOMETIMES, IT CAN BE DIFFICULT TO KNOW HOW TO BALANCE INDEPENDENCE WITH *INTER*DEPENDENCE, WHICH IS THE HEALTHY RELIANCE ON A SUPPORTIVE CIRCLE OF PEOPLE IN ORDER TO KEEP LEARNING AND GROWING.**

difficulty separating from the family or thriving in college or at their first job. They may have difficulty navigating relationships or creating better opportunities for themselves. They may find it tough to achieve some semblance of financial independence and may need to overly rely on family members to solve problems. Other common characteristics of a failure to launch include the following:

- Poor or inconsistent work ethic
- Low levels of motivation or willpower
- Low resilience in the face of problems or stress
- High expectations of others to take care of them
- Avoidance of responsibilities or making excuses to get out of obligations
- Lack of realistic long-term goals
- Lack of daily living skills for early adulthood (e.g., financial literacy, basic cooking and cleaning competency)
- Irritable mood coupled with symptoms of depression or anxiety

Well-meaning parents can help children develop a healthy sense of independence and interdependence by considering these tips:

1. ***Decide on and communicate healthy boundaries.*** Teens and preteens should have some responsibilities at home and regularly contribute to household tasks and chores. Determine age-appropriate tasks for your child, and let them know that these are the expectations they should meet as they are being provided a home to live in, food on the table, and other necessities (e.g., school supplies) and luxuries (e.g., smartphones, video games, weekend outings with friends).

2. ***Involve your teen in exploring their interests and skills.*** Ask your teen what types of hobbies they want to try or what skills they'd like to develop. To help engage them in these exercises, consider asking them to take a personality inventory (like the Myers–Briggs) or a skills and interest-development survey (such as the Campbell Interest and Skill Survey or the Strong Interest Inventory) so that they can learn more about themselves and decide what areas they'd like to explore.

3. ***Resist the urge to overprotect them.*** No parent wants to see their child struggle or face adversity, but try to reframe these as opportunities for them to develop resilience and problem-solving skills. When you see them going through a difficult time, instead of solving the problem for them, ask how you can help. Max has some great language to guide parents—check out page 32 for her helpful "comfort or solution" question. Whether it's lending a listening ear or helping them to brainstorm strategies to deal with the problem, some level of support is helpful and appropriate—as long as you don't completely take control of the situation and try to solve their problems for them.

4. ***Do regular postcrisis analysis.*** After particularly stressful times, sit down with your teen or preteen and review how they approached the problem, providing positive reinforcement and validation for good coping strategies they used and asking them to reflect on what areas they can improve on in the future. This type of postcrisis analysis is great for building self-confidence and rehearsing other tactics that might come in handy in the future, as well as for avoiding the same pitfalls in a similar situation that might arise later.

own qualifications. "If so-and-so was the valedictorian and didn't get in, I'm never going to get in!"

The truth is, getting into school is about a lot more than just grades and scores. But you can easily get so wrapped up in all the numbers that you can no longer focus on the big picture. Sometimes it's hard to remember that colleges use a holistic approach for their admissions process. You can also get stuck comparing your extracurricular activities to others when you might have a great story to tell in the essay. You can get obsessed to the point where it's not healthy and get close to or even reach a breaking point. And who knows . . . maybe it's all a buildup of those pressures that started so many years ago when you were eight or twelve or whatever age. I think it's more than just one class or even one year being tough. We may have youth and energy on our side, but we don't have endurance or perspective, really, and we've been taught to tie so much of our self-worth to our school performance.

HOW TO OFFER SUPPORT

I recently took the ACTs for the first time. It was a tough test even though I had been studying for it for an entire year. When I found out my score was thirty (four points short of my goal score), I felt completely defeated. I was already so mentally exhausted from preparing for finals and AP tests and everything else I had to do for school that adding this major disappointment just broke me. I couldn't handle it.

My mom came in at 7:00 a.m. to tell me that my score came out, but she didn't have access to the website. We logged on together, and when we saw my score, she said, "You can bump your score up four points. You have the power, whether you realize it or not."

Now, my mom is usually good at making me feel better about things, but this was really not what I needed to hear. Basically, it felt like she was saying that I didn't get the score because I didn't work hard enough . . . but I felt like I had worked as hard as I possibly could. So how could I possibly do better than what was maybe my best?

I think at that moment, I also felt annoyed that I didn't have a little time to mourn falling short of my goal. I had put so much pressure on myself to get the score I needed, and I really felt like my entire self-worth was built around this test score and my grades.

At times like this, parents don't always know what to say, and that's OK—they're human too. What I would have liked to hear is something like, "I've seen how hard you have worked. Just because you didn't get the score you wanted does not negate the year and hours you spent studying for this test, and I am so proud of you." Maybe later, once she gave me time to process the score, she could say, "Sure, it's not the score you wanted, but you're going to get the score you wanted, and if you don't, again, it's not the end of the world."

My experience isn't like everyone else's, but as a kid who has made it through some tough middle school years and is pushing through my final high school years, I can share some of the tactics that would have been helpful for my parents to use during some of these challenging times.

ASK, "DO YOU WANT COMFORT OR A SOLUTION?"

This is one of my favorite questions that I have picked up from many people. You can use it with anyone who's going through something; I use it for my friends, anyone I'm dating, and even with my parents sometimes.

For the ACT score scenario, had my mom asked this question of me, I think I would have told her I wanted comfort. That response would have been about being on my side, with my mom saying something like, "That was a stupid test. That was a specifically hard ACT. This test doesn't define you. This test is not going to determine whether you get into college or not—because it's not the whole picture."

If I wanted a solution, her response would be more like, "OK, how are we going to study for this? What part do you need to revisit and restudy? Let's figure out a plan to get the score you want and know you can get."

I really think this question allows you to be a better helper, even if the person you ask picks the third option: "Neither—I just want to be left alone." Even if that's the answer, what's needed has been

"I wish they'd realize that staying in my room a lot isn't a crime. Hello, some of my friends are doing drugs."

—C., Maryland, eighteen

communicated, and that's big. And if the third option is the case, the question can always be revisited when the person is ready to talk. Had my mom asked me this that morning, we would not have gotten into a fight about my score, and I would have felt much better about it.

ESTABLISH PERSPECTIVE . . . WHILE REMEMBERING THAT THINGS ARE DIFFERENT NOW.

When you're in school, *especially* middle school and high school, it can feel like it's your whole world and it's going to be your world forever. A little perspective from parents could be helpful. No guarantees, though, because it's hard for kids to see themselves existing outside of the school bubble, but it is totally worth a shot. You could try pointing out that this thing—whatever it is—that feels so big now isn't going to matter later in your life or share that you had something similar happen and it was tough at the time, but you got through it. The problem with parents when they want to tell a story to relate to their kids is that it's tough for them to leave out a little judgment or condescension—or what might come across that way. I can totally hear my dad saying, "Well, when *I* took it, the college test was much harder, but I survived, and so will you." Comments like that aren't going to help as much.

My dad really does say things to me that begin with, "When I was in high school" (or college or med school), and I find it really hard to relate to what comes next. I'm pretty sure that when he was in high school, it was a thousand times easier to get good grades. He didn't have social media or tons of extracurricular obligations, and he barely had an AP class—they came out during his senior year in high school. So when I'm taking a bunch of AP classes and he took one, but he's telling me that I just need to work harder and focus more, it's hard for it to come across as helpful even if that's the intention.

"I wish my parents let me be independent. If I need help, I'll ask. And please don't do things for me that I can do or have started doing."

—G., Yorkshire (UK), fourteen

ACKNOWLEDGE THE WORK THEY'RE DOING.

If you are working hard as a student and your parents see that work, it's nice for it to be acknowledged. It doesn't have to be anything more than "We see you, and we acknowledge the amount of effort you're putting in." That's way better than "You could work harder," when it would be almost impossible for that to happen unless more hours were added to each day.

LET YOUR KID TAKE A BREAK.

I get that attendance is important and you don't want to miss out on any lessons, but sometimes kids seriously need a mental break. Adults can call in "sick" even when they're not just to reset and recover, and kids need that time too. If my mom can tell that I am super overwhelmed or stressed out, she has helped me find ways to talk to my teachers about skipping an assignment or turning it in late. Or she's been OK with me taking a mental health day off from school. Every once in a while, a gift like that can mean the world to a schoolkid. If you don't allow it, they're probably going to find a way themselves, so why not be the one to get the credit for letting them take a needed break? You might also help them avoid a total meltdown.

HELP THEM GET EXTRA HELP . . . IF THAT'S WHAT IS NEEDED.

When your kids are not understanding a topic or it's just really difficult, they might need extra help, and parents can assist in providing that by setting up after-school sessions with a teacher or getting their teen to spend time with a friend who really understands the topic and can maybe explain it better. Parents can also get their teens help from a tutor, if that's an option. Of course, it's important to remember that in some cases, it's not about the difficulty of the material or concept but the outrageous amount of work required in a class. Tutors or extra time with teachers won't help with being overloaded with work.

HELP THEM HAVE THE RESOURCES TO PLAN OUT THEIR WEEK.

When you're a kid, no one really teaches you time-management skills—it's kind of just like, "Here's all the work you have to do—figure out how to get it done in time!" You might consider helping your teen get set up for success . . . without micromanaging. Some ways to do this include encouraging them to use a planner and suggesting that they not set up a lot of activities for weeks when they have a lot of schoolwork due.

One of the resources you offer them might be yourself—just being the person they can rant to or cry to. Don't forget that this is an essential way to offer support.

COMMUNICATE ABOUT WHAT'S REALLY GOING ON.

This goes for both parents and kids. A lot of parents know when their child is struggling, but sometimes you don't know what the issue is or what the situation is specifically, which can change how effective any help you offer will be. If you think it's because they don't understand something and don't want to ask for help, but it's actually that they're having a really hard time mentally, then you're going to give the wrong suggestions and find the wrong help—you're going to get a tutor instead of a therapist. Hopefully, simply asking will reveal the answer. Explaining that you're not asking to judge but rather to help could provide the nudge that's needed. Your kid has to feel that they can trust you to communicate openly, and they have to be able to say, "I hope you're willing to help me without judgment." A lot of kids will keep stuff in or make up other stories if they feel that being honest about school struggles will only result in judgment and scolding.

DR. JUDY'S NOTES

PARENTAL MONITORING: HOW TO HAVE A CLOSE AND HEALTHY RELATIONSHIP WITH YOUR TEEN WITHOUT SUFFOCATING THEM

Do you know where your teen is right now? Where they usually are after school or on weekends? What do they tell you they're up to—and what do you think they're really up to? Who are their closest friends, and how do they like spending their time?

The teen years are a time of natural risk-taking and boundary pushing as adolescents try to figure out who they are and what they're made of. Even the most well-behaved kids might succumb to peer pressure, make bad decisions, and lie to try to stay out of trouble with parents and teachers.

There are many lively discussions about whether or not there is one "right" way to parent. I think there are many ways to parent well, and most suggested methods include some emphasis on high levels of parental monitoring in order to create positive outcomes for teens. These outcomes are well established in the literature and include lower rates of delinquency and substance abuse and higher self-esteem and academic achievement.

> **THE TEEN YEARS ARE A TIME OF NATURAL RISK-TAKING AND BOUNDARY PUSHING AS ADOLESCENTS TRY TO FIGURE OUT WHO THEY ARE AND WHAT THEY'RE MADE OF.**

YOU DON'T WANT YOUR TEEN TO START THINKING OF YOUR CONVERSATIONS WITH THEM AS PUNISHMENT.

Parental monitoring can be defined as a set of correlated parenting behaviors involving attention to and tracking of the child's whereabouts, activities, and adaptations to their constantly changing environmental demands. This does not mean following every single move your teen makes or interrogating them about their whereabouts until they tell you to screw off. Rather, it involves regular check-ins, with open lines of communication, that enable important discussions in as naturalistic of an environment (i.e., using naturally occurring situations rather than posing "what-if" theoretical scenarios) as possible. You don't want your teen to start thinking of your conversations with them as punishment, so it is important to build in positive reinforcement and incentives as a part of your regular discussions.

The following are my best tips for how to instill a culture of naturalistic parental monitoring with your teen:

1. *Establish regular quality time on a daily basis.* Having a regularly scheduled time where family members participate in a joint activity with undivided attention is one of the major keys to setting up an environment for routine conversations about what your teen did that day, what issues they're dealing with, or what their interests of the moment are. One easy way to do this is to establish regular mealtimes where all members of the family must participate, with no electronic device distractions (I like to tell parents to set out a box where everyone drops in their cell phones before sitting down at the table for dinner).

2. *Open up a bidirectional channel of communication.* This is a space in which your teen can air their grievances

to you and also ask you questions about yourself; as a result, any conversations you initiate about how they are spending their time may not feel like an interrogation to them. Let your teen know that your door is always open if they want to ask you anything. Be prepared to disclose some details about your own hobbies, friendships, and how you spend your free time. That way, when you ask them what they're up to, it feels less like an investigation and more like a reciprocal conversation where your teen can also experience some agency and take the opportunity to know you better.

LET YOUR TEEN KNOW THAT YOUR DOOR IS ALWAYS OPEN IF THEY WANT TO ASK YOU ANYTHING. BE PREPARED TO DISCLOSE SOME DETAILS ABOUT YOUR OWN HOBBIES, FRIENDSHIPS, AND HOW YOU SPEND YOUR FREE TIME.

3. ***Begin a family meetings routine.*** Family meetings are my favorite way to help enhance communication and foster closeness among family members. Set aside thirty minutes a week where all family members come together to discuss a variety of topics relevant to the family. This should include both positive and not-so-positive things, such as where the family would like to plan their next vacation, how they want to spend their upcoming long weekend, how to manage a recent conflict between family members, or discussions about new family rules or chore assignments. Everyone in the family can take on a rotating role, such as the snack provider, the note taker, the agenda setter, the meeting leader, et cetera. It's a great way to practice open and assertive communication and to

allow a routine forum where parents can check in with their teens about what they're up to and how they're spending their time outside the home.

4. ***Remember your role as a parent while maintaining empathy and closeness with your teen.*** You don't have to be your teen's best friend (at least, not right now, at this developmental stage), but you can be a person who they see as a confidant and someone they can rely on for support, while at the same time maintaining your role as the parent, which sometimes requires you to lay down the law and be the rule maker. It can be hard to toe this line, but one helpful tip is to explain the rationale behind your decisions, and remind them that when you hand down discipline, it's for their protection rather than purely to punish them for the heck of it. Even if your teen says they don't want to talk about a problem that you can clearly see is troubling them, don't take no for an answer. Let them know that it's OK if they don't feel like talking about it at this moment but that you will be checking in with them regularly if they change their mind. Again, a bit of self-disclosure can be helpful. Teens may think that you don't understand what they're going through, so letting them know that you struggle with occasional anxiety or have difficulty managing your stress or friendships can show them that you can relate to their situation, which can lead to better communication.

> YOU DON'T HAVE TO BE YOUR TEEN'S BEST FRIEND . . . BUT YOU CAN BE A PERSON WHO THEY SEE AS A CONFIDANT AND SOMEONE THEY CAN RELY ON FOR SUPPORT, WHILE AT THE SAME TIME MAINTAINING YOUR ROLE AS THE PARENT.

It can be tough to have a good relationship with your parents during your preteen and teen years. My parents and I have managed to maintain pretty healthy relationships through even these more difficult years. Here are some things they've done that I think have helped make that the case (I'm not saying these are going to work for everyone, but they've helped in our family).

THEY TREAT ME WITH RESPECT.

My parents treat me—and have always kind of treated me—like an adult. They respect me and expect respect in return.

THEY TRUST ME.

And they trust me 100 percent. They are super open about their lives, which is why I'm super open about mine. And I trust them not to weaponize things I tell them, meaning I know they won't use them against me. I also know that we have privacy and that they will keep things to themselves. And I trust that they won't tell my siblings if I don't want them to, or their friends, or whoever's not in on the secret (which might even be one of them).

One thing I really appreciate is the fact that they trusted me first—and I would have to do something to lose it—instead of starting off by not trusting me and making me

> ONE THING I REALLY APPRECIATE IS THE FACT THAT THEY TRUSTED ME FIRST—AND I WOULD HAVE TO DO SOMETHING TO LOSE IT—INSTEAD OF STARTING OFF BY NOT TRUSTING ME AND MAKING ME EARN IT.

earn it. That felt like real trust, and I honored it by not lying to them. Obviously, if you give your parents a reason not to trust you, that's something else. Not only do parents have to expect that their kids are not lying and doing shady stuff, but the kids also can't lie and do shady stuff. It's definitely a deal you both have to agree to.

THEY APOLOGIZE.

One of the things I really appreciate about my parents is that if they're wrong, they apologize. I think some parents believe that they're always right because they are the adults. But I think that can make you feel really disconnected from your parent if they're wrong but don't acknowledge it. I don't mean this in a disrespectful way, but parents do make mistakes.

My mom is especially good with this. She apologizes as soon as she knows she's wrong. She's not one of those parents who backpedals away from what she said in order to avoid an apology. She'll say, "Oh, I'm sorry. That was my fault. Keep going." This really makes me feel like a valued member of the relationship and family.

THEY TELL US THEY'RE NOT PERFECT.

They definitely tell my siblings and me all the time how they're not perfect, they're trying, and they're learning with us, which I think is really important because sometimes it feels like parents try to create this impression that they have a flawless strategy for everything, but sometimes they really have no idea what they're doing.

THEY'RE NOT PERFECT, THEY'RE TRYING, AND THEY'RE LEARNING WITH US.

Especially with your first or oldest children, it's always a learning experience . . . but if you can learn together rather than separately, then maybe you can grow together too. You will not only get a better understanding of your kids for the next time around, but it will also bring you closer together. And we do that really well in the Dubrow family.

Another thing I appreciate about my mom is that she will think about what she would have wished her parents would have done in a given scenario. And she'll really try to remember what she felt like as a kid or a teen, which means she'll try to give me and my siblings a break and let us be kids. This means that sometimes we're going to mess up— we will forget stuff, and we might not be totally open about things 100 percent of the time. She's been there. She knows that sometimes kids act like kids.

My mom makes sure I know that she's accepting and understanding by telling me that we have a judgment-free zone and that I can always come to her, but that I don't have to. What's funny is that this kind of no-pressure offer has made it so that I *want* to tell her things because (a) I know she's not going to judge me, (b) I know she knows a lot more than I do, and (c) I know that she is going to help me instead of telling me what I did wrong and scolding me for doing something I wasn't supposed to. Instead of that, she'll tell me what I can do better next time.

MY MOM MAKES SURE I KNOW THAT SHE'S ACCEPTING AND UNDERSTANDING BY TELLING ME THAT WE HAVE A JUDGMENT-FREE ZONE AND THAT I CAN ALWAYS COME TO HER, BUT THAT I DON'T HAVE TO.

Here's a hypothetical example of what I mean. Let's say that if I drank alcohol, which I don't, but let's say if I went out and got super drunk at a party, and I called her saying, "Mom, I'm so drunk, and I can't get home, and blah, blah, blah, blah. And we're stuck, and no one's really left at this party except a few creepy guys." Instead of saying, "YOU'RE DRUNK, are you kidding me? You're in so much trouble." She would say, "Where are you? I'll come get you right now." Of course, we'd have to talk about it later, and it wouldn't just be acceptable, but I wouldn't be in trouble for making a mistake. Instead, we would learn together about how I could do things differently the next time.

The problem with some parent–teen relationships is that a lot of kids won't tell their parents when they're in trouble, because they're afraid of getting punished for it. So if they try that approach once and they're reprimanded or grounded, of course the kid is going to think, "The next time I'm in trouble, I'm not going to call you. I'm just going to deal with the situation," but then they are going to be in *real* trouble. Now, I'm not saying that there

IF YOU NEVER LET YOUR KIDS FAIL, THEY WILL NEVER LEARN. YOU NEED TO TRUST YOUR KIDS ENOUGH, AND HOPE THAT YOU TAUGHT THEM WELL, TO ALLOW THEM THE FREEDOM TO MESS UP.

shouldn't be consequences to your kid's actions; I'm saying that anger should not be your first response. If you never let your kids fail, they will never learn. You need to trust your kids enough, and hope that you taught them well, to allow them the freedom to mess up.

THEY'VE STOPPED FORCING ME TO BE BEST FRIENDS WITH ALL MY SIBLINGS.

My parents used to put a lot of pressure on me and my three siblings to be best friends—and mostly me since I'm the oldest girl.

This is something that I don't think is realistic because the only factors that bond you together as siblings are genetics and living in a house together for a certain amount of time. Neither of these factors means you have similar music tastes, similar interests, similar personalities, or similar passions.

Often, there are also conflicting pressures—on one side, the pressure to be best friends with your siblings, and on the other side, the pressure to compete with each other in grades or sports or other areas of accomplishment. This can create this sense that you need to be better than your siblings rather than wanting them to succeed alongside you, and it also introduces resistance to being friends with your siblings—if you are all trying to get your parents' attention or trying to "win" and be the best child, you are naturally going to feel at odds with one another. I think parents, my parents included, can accidentally fuel these complicated sibling emotions.

Over time, my parents have realized that we will always be siblings who love each other—nothing will ever change that. They've started to give us more space to be ourselves and discover our own identities. And they have accepted that it's way more likely that we will all be super tight when we get older and are more mature. It's hard when you're going through different stages of life and school years to be totally aligned. Oh—and they got us a dog! Which is an awesome, organic way to bring kids of all ages together.

WHAT PARENTS SHOULD KNOW

- School pressure—the pressure to do well academically— is the **number-one stressor** in most kids' lives.
- The pressure can be overwhelming and intense, and it can definitely **intensify** any mental health issues your teen may have.
- Even if you think comparing your school experience to your child's is helpful, it may not be, especially if the tone is condescending. Performance standards are extremely high, and the competition is intense; things *are* different, so maybe **try acknowledging this difference** when relating to your kid's experience.
- Open, **nonjudgmental communication** and **mutual respect** can go a long way in helping both parents and teens make it through high-pressure years.

WARNING SIGNS YOUR TEEN MIGHT NEED EXTRA SUPPORT

With so much going on, it can be difficult to see the signs that your teen needs extra TLC from you—and in some cases, professionals to help get them back on track. Here are some signs to pay attention to:

- A significant drop in grades and/or frequent tardies or absences
- Lack of interest in activities they used to enjoy
- Difficulties concentrating or making simple, daily decisions
- Decrease in self-care and personal hygiene and/or excessive sleeping or persistently low energy
- Disengagement from family interactions or their social circle
- Notable change in appetite and eating behaviors (starving self or binge eating)
- Showing excessive worry about the future
- Increased irritability at minor annoyances and/or increased crying or temper outbursts
- Saying out loud, "This is too much," or "I can't take it anymore"*
- Exhibiting self-harm (e.g., cutting or burning self on skin) or expressing thoughts like "I wish I weren't here anymore"*

If you observe more than two or three of these signs (*note that the last two likely warrant immediate attention and referral to a professional) and they linger for more than a couple weeks, talk with your teen. Share your observations without jumping to any conclusions or offering your own interpretations of their behavior (e.g., "I've noticed you've been sleeping a lot," *not* "Is this because you're depressed?"). Then, ask them what they think based on what you just shared with them. After listening to their reflections, ask them how you can help. Have them come up with their own ideas of what you can do to assist them, then, offer some ideas of your own (which may include directing them to professional help). Try to use reflective listening during these conversations: summarize their thoughts (so they have a chance to correct any misperceptions you might have) and then offer a statement of empathy and solidarity. For example, "I hear that you're telling me school has been more stressful than ever lately, and I can empathize with that feeling of constant pressure."

If you find that your teen may need professional help, a list of helpful resources are provided in the next chapter. Additional informational resources that might be helpful for you and your teen are located on page 167.

Anxiety

All I want to do is cry

But I am so sick of crying

I'm so sick of being out of control of my own emotions

Of not being able to have harmony
between my thoughts and mind

I don't even know I need to cry until I do

I don't want to be weak

I don't want to have to ask for help

How is it fair that I live in fear?

While others laugh

I put myself in situations
that I can't handle

Because I should be able to

And I can

I just don't want to

I want to give up   Turn around   Go home

not have to worry anymore

Silence my mind

But that's unreasonable

CHAPTER 2

ANXIETY

Can't Just "Snap Out of It"

When I was in middle school, I started to feel super anxious a lot of the time. I had major anxiety about school pressure and the need to excel academically, and I began to experience social anxiety specifically. This made it so that whenever I was in front of my friends or peers, I was so anxious that I was going to say the wrong thing or that I was going to get laughed at for something I did or said or wore . . . or whatever. It got so bad that I didn't want to hang out with people, and I didn't want to go anywhere because I was constantly afraid of being embarrassed or made fun of.

It's not really surprising that I started to feel anxious during middle school because it was the worst time in my life. (I'm sure plenty of adults reading this might think, "Oh please, you just wait." But I'm seventeen, and in my short-ish life so far, I can without a doubt say those three or four years stand out for their awfulness.)

I dealt with these issues for a little while on my own, but then I talked to my parents, who helped me arrange to see a therapist. At first, I was nervous to ask my parents about therapy. I didn't want them to worry that I needed help. This just goes to show that even though we have come such a far way, there is still a stigma around mental health and therapy. Why should a kid feel nervous about asking for help in getting through a tough time?

It was only after I started going to therapy and talking about it that some of my friends started mentioning their own therapists. This made me feel so much more secure in my decision to get real help, and the bonus was that I could talk to my friends about my experiences. I didn't feel alone, and it actually became a joke in my friend group. We would laugh and say, "I have therapy at 4:00. Want to hang out after?" I loved that it wasn't a secret, and we were able to bond about our shared dedication to bettering ourselves.

What's cool about modern therapy is there are so many ways to access it. Teens can get support in person or via text or video. And there are a lot of ways to find affordable therapy. If you aren't willing or able to help, you can direct your teen to federally or state-funded programs—there's information on these in the Resources section at the end of the book. (Btw, I realize that not being *willing* to help and not being *able* to help are totally different things, but the resources for your child may ultimately be the same.)

GETTING DIAGNOSED

I was ultimately diagnosed with social anxiety, general anxiety, and emetophobia (fear of vomiting). These conditions all have fears and challenges that overlap, but I can share a little about how I've experienced each. I'm definitely not a mental health professional, so these aren't clinical definitions; they're more like how I've understood my

"I wish my parents could be more understanding—I may <u>look</u> OK, but internally, I am not. Looks can be deceiving."
—M., California, sixteen

symptoms to be a reflection of different disorders. I think being able to describe these has helped me—not to mention my family and closest friends—understand more about anxiety.

SOCIAL ANXIETY

My anxiety really began with social anxiety. When I was about eleven, I became overcome with fear that I was saying or was going to say the wrong thing in front of my friends and that I was going to get laughed at or talked about later. I was so afraid of it that I didn't want to hang out with people and didn't want to go anywhere; I hated leaving the house. All because I was scared of being embarrassed or made fun of. I know this sounds so silly to some people, but once these kinds of thoughts start taking over in your head, they are really powerful . . . and you feel powerless against them.

GENERAL ANXIETY

What started with social anxiety eventually grew into what I would call *everything anxiety*, but it's called *general anxiety*. For me, this involved irrational fears that created lingering, constant anxiety about *everything* (except for test taking, which is strange since I'm obsessed with my grades). I started feeling scared that everyone around me was going to die, and I'd have to say "I love you" when I'd leave a room or hang up the phone.

Mostly, general anxiety made me feel like I was always just a second away from some terrible tragedy. I was scared of dying, that people I loved were going to die, that the worst was just about to happen all the time. And it became a cycle that sort of shut down my life in a big way. For example, if a friend was having a birthday party, I would feel scared of dying in an accident on the way to the party . . . and then, even if I envisioned getting to the party alive, I was terrified of being at the party around people, where I was probably going to say something stupid. It was all worry, fear, anxiety . . . and then it actually got worse (before it got better, and it does get better).

Around the same time, I went on a trip with my family and got food poisoning or something on the flight home. I was so sick while stuck on this plane. I had never experienced this before, and I didn't know I was about to vomit. I ended up throwing up in the middle of the aisle while walking to tell my mom that I was feeling hot. This was *before* the plane had taken off, so there was an entire flight and car ride to endure before getting home.

It was so awful to be stuck so far away from home and not be able to do anything about it. It was traumatizing. This sparked my irrational fear of not only being terrified of throwing up (and the fear of just doing it everywhere I go) but also not being able to control where I was. At first, I was afraid to drive because I didn't want to feel sick and be alone. I then came to realize that if I could control where the car was going, I could always go home or stop. This has led to a need for me to be in control of many things in my life, but it helps my anxiety to have a distinct, unchanging plan.

I was so afraid of having to throw up and not being able to get to a bathroom that I started feeling like I didn't want to eat. I would only eat bars or boxed mac 'n' cheese, and I would constantly ask my mom if something was likely to give me food poisoning.

I found out that this is a specific phobia, called *emetophobia*— literally "the fear of vomiting"—and it's not totally uncommon. In fact, I've seen a lot on TikTok of people having this exact same problem. And not to say that I'm glad other people have this issue, but I was so relieved to hear other people share their experiences because it feels so random. There's a certain calm feeling you get when you find out other people have the same fear as you—at least you're not alone!

I had started working through a lot of these issues with therapy, meds, et cetera—I will go into more of that a little later in the chapter—but then this little thing called COVID-19 hit, and it pushed me and everyone else in the world into their homes. I didn't have to go to school or anywhere, and this made all my anxieties come back big time. To the point where I didn't want to go back to school when it reopened . . . and so I didn't—I just stayed with online school.

Ultimately, I ended up pretty much not leaving the house for almost an entire year, which was really bad because I even started to feel like my safe space was getting smaller and smaller. I started feeling like I couldn't even leave my room—I actually had a panic attack going to the kitchen. It was truly debilitating.

But I had my therapist, who helped me work through it, and it's gotten a lot better. I began doing simple things, like driving through my neighborhood alone. I then worked up to going to drive-through restaurants and eventually my friends' houses. I still have anxiety going to a lot of places, but exposure to these situations has helped me a lot.

WHAT MAKES ANXIETY SO HARD TO DEAL WITH

One of the toughest things about anxiety is how hard it is to describe to people who don't experience it themselves. Imagine trying to explain an emotion to someone who's never felt that emotion— adding in the fact that you don't even really understand the emotion or why you're feeling it. Specifically, it's like trying to tell someone who's never been in love what it feels like to be in love, except instead of being awesome, it sucks.

The experience of anxiety often goes like this: You have no idea why this is happening to you and can't explain why you just started having a panic attack, but it's happening, and there's no turning back. You have no idea if it's anxiety (but it's always anxiety) or something

TEEN TALK

"Generally, we aren't faking anxiety—we are just bad at describing what is wrong."

—D., California, sixteen

DR. JUDY'S NOTES

UNDERSTANDING AND IDENTIFYING ANXIETY IN YOUNG PEOPLE

Anxiety is one of the most commonly diagnosed mental health concerns in children and teens. Approximately 4.4 million youth between the ages of three and seventeen are diagnosed with an anxiety disorder each year, and data suggest that anxiety conditions among children and teens have increased over time. Teens between the ages of twelve and seventeen have the highest rates of anxiety (up to 10.5–11 percent compared with 6.5–7 percent in children aged six to eleven). This is likely related, in part, to the stresses of transitioning to middle school and high school and the increasing social, academic, and peer pressures, as well as struggles with identity and self-esteem development, that often happen during this crucial time. Youth who experience a more negative family environment, those who experience academic difficulties or failures in early elementary school years, and those who deal with significant loss and grief are more at risk for anxiety symptoms.

Despite its prevalence, 40 percent of youth with anxiety issues don't receive any professional treatment. Some parents assume treatment for their child (or themselves) would be too costly or would not be covered by insurance. It is important to know that treatment does not have to be costly; there are many sliding-fee-scale clinics, university-run clinics, and other community clinics that offer free or low-cost services. However, self-stigma regarding the experience of mental health symptoms and misunderstandings about the professional mental health

ANXIETY, LIKE ALL MENTAL HEALTH CONCERNS, OCCURS ON A SPECTRUM.

sector might cause people to be reluctant to seek help. This is concerning because treatment can help reduce the intensity and frequency of symptoms and also teach important coping skills so that teens can better manage their symptoms and stressors and continue to live happy, productive, and prosocial lives. I am so glad Max mentioned the value that therapy has had for her; she might still struggle with anxiety symptoms sometimes, but therapy has definitely given her more confidence and coping strategies to deal with symptoms when they arise.

Anxiety, like all mental health concerns, occurs on a spectrum; some anxiety is normal and can even be beneficial at times. Most ideas about anxiety consider the costs and benefits to be on a U-shaped curve and adhere to the Goldilocks Rule—in other words, a "just-right" rule for the experience of anxiety. A little anxiety can be helpful in some situations, such as the mild nervousness one may experience while preparing for a big presentation for class or the moderate anxiety about an upcoming test that might lead the person to study more, which in turn helps them to do well on test day. No anxiety about anything in life whatsoever can also be a bit of a problem—a person with no anxiety is likely to be unmotivated, have difficulty reaching goals, or be indifferent to social cues and put less effort into relationships that might benefit their well-being.

Although anxiety symptoms differ from person to person, here are some of the common signs to watch for in children and teens:

Physical signs

- Complaints of bodily aches (head, stomach) and tense muscles with no medical reason

- Changes in eating habits (overeating or expressing no appetite) and sleep routines (sleeping too much or too little)
- Appearing agitated, hyperactive, or distracted

Behavioral signs

- School refusal or making excuses to skip classes and other social functions
- Avoidance of family members and withdrawal from friends
- Anger outbursts or overreactions to minor stresses
- Excessive approval-seeking behaviors
- Compulsive behaviors, such as obsessing about little details, frequent handwashing, or arranging and rearranging things

Emotional signs

- Crying easily or becoming cranky for no reason
- Exhibiting self-doubt and expressing low self-esteem
- Having difficulty handling criticism
- Expressing fears and phobias
- Worrying about many different things, including things in the far future

If your teen experiences any of these symptoms, let them know they are not alone. You can find a trusted person (like another family member, a teacher, or a family friend) for them to talk to about their experiences, or look into professional support with therapists and psychiatrists that is confidential and can help them manage their symptoms. There are many scientific treatments for anxiety, several of which do not require taking medication (such as cognitive-behavioral therapy). People generally start to feel better within a few weeks of therapy, whether they go to psychotherapy or begin taking medications to reduce anxiety symptoms.

"I wish my parents understood that I'm not making myself feel this way, so saying 'Stop being anxious' doesn't help."

—C., Florida, fifteen

else. You try saying, "I feel like I can't breathe," and someone's saying, "OK, well, did you eat something?" You try to say, "You don't get it," except you're too busy chasing control of your heartbeat, and it's way faster than you.

On the surface, it seems like a simple concept. When you get stressed or put in a situation where you're uncomfortable, your body naturally responds with anxiety. Most people—including people with anxiety—get that, but what's hard for others to understand is how difficult it is to control and how much you've tried to understand how or why it manifests.

All of this can make anxiety very isolating, which is really tough because it's already something that makes you feel so alone. What has made me feel less alone lately is the fact that I have more friends who have developed anxiety, not only from the pandemic but also just from school and stuff. Not to say I'm glad they're struggling too, but it's something we can talk to each other about.

This is pretty much the opposite of when I first started having serious anxiety. At that time, which was during ninth grade (when it got really bad), I lost a lot of friends because they didn't get it. They thought I didn't want to hang out with them or I didn't want to come to whatever they were doing, and even though I tried to explain that it wasn't them but my anxiety, it didn't matter. They would end up getting mad, and sadly, I probably would have responded the same way if I hadn't known what it felt like.

When it comes to talking to my parents, I guess I'm lucky in the sense that both of my parents have experienced some type of anxiety, so there's not a complete lack of understanding. My anxiety is more intense than what they've experienced, but at least they don't look at me like I'm an alien when I tell them what's going on. My sisters, who are three and seven years younger than me, don't really make a big deal out of my anxiety, which I am thankful for. My twin brother, Nicky, however, tries very hard to understand. I will come to him and tell him how I don't want to go places, and he will assure me that it will be fun and that he can always pick me up if I need him to. He has always been my biggest supporter and helps me any way he can.

THERAPY AND OTHER TOOLS FOR DEALING WITH ANXIETY

I started going to therapy in early 2020, which was game changing. But it's not the only thing that has made a difference for me. Here are some strategies I've used to address my anxiety.

THERAPY

Definitely therapy. I feel like some people think therapy is weird or just not something they would be into. You are, after all, talking to a stranger, at least at first. I was cautious to tell my therapist my whole story at the beginning because I didn't want her to think I was just being dramatic. I have come to realize that not only is she trained in my exact areas of anxiety, but she works with many other patients who deal with the exact same thing.

As I have continued with therapy, I have gotten closer to my therapist and am able to tell her all about my life without the fear that she will tell someone else. It's like having a best friend who legally can't tell

TEEN TALK

"I wish that every parent with the means to do so would offer a therapist to their kid."

—J., Arizona, seventeen

"You can't just 'snap out of" anxiety. You need space and support from your parents to get through it."

—N., South Africa, nineteen

TEEN TALK

anyone what you say; it's amazing. (No drama ever!) I love my therapist, and that's strange for me to say because I hate everyone. OK, I don't hate everyone, but I have trust issues stemming from middle school, and it's really hard for me to feel totally comfortable talking to someone. Yet I trust my therapist completely, and she's been so key to helping me work through my anxiety issues.

I can't even explain how nice it is to have someone say to you, "Yeah, well, what you're feeling is completely normal. Here are the tools I have that can help, and let's deal with it." It's so relieving to hear something like this when you've been struggling with anxiety and everyone around you is just as lost as you are. This is the benefit of going to a licensed therapist who isn't just guessing but can actually provide guidance.

The other thing that's great about a therapist is that you don't need to get into the deep stuff every session; sometimes it's kind of a nice way even just to vent. Being able to talk about surface-level, annoying stuff helps you feel more comfortable getting into the uncomfortable stuff. And yes, sometimes kids just need to vent too.

MINDSET SHIFT: 5-4-3-2-1

My understanding of this method is that it is intended to ground you from your anxiety. You practice it by using your senses, which feels like a way to distract your brain. If I'm feeling anxious somewhere, I will find five things that I see, four things I can touch, three things I can hear, two things I can smell, and one thing I can taste. These don't have to be literal—for example, you can notice a perfume bottle nearby and count it as a scent without sniffing it—and it still works. Honestly, every time I use this method, the experience is a little bit different, but it still works. I love it because it is easy to do wherever you are and is very discreet.

SUPPORT SYSTEM

I think having a support system is really important because sometimes just talking about it makes the anxiety not as bad. I know the tendency is to want to shut people out because you feel like no one's going to understand, but it's not about understanding—it's just having someone who can say, "You're going to be OK."

If I'm in the car on my way to a party and I have a panic attack, I know I can reach out to my mom, my best friend, or an older friend whom I love like a sister and just say, "I feel like I'm going to throw up . . . I am so scared . . . I hate this . . . I want to go home . . . blah, blah, blah." And then I'll hear back something like, "First of all, I can come pick you up. Second of all, you're fine. And third, you're not going to die. You know? Everything is OK." This is really effective in helping me feel better, and because I know that, I make sure that this is the kind of messaging I send to my friends who are also dealing with anxiety.

If I am dealing with anxiety of my own, I now understand that I have to be willing to communicate what I can about it. And if I know someone who is dealing with anxiety, I have to be willing to listen or just be the one to answer the phone. If I'm having an off day, I'll call one of my friends and say, "I'm having such bad anxiety right now. Can you distract me?" This helps me a lot. I'll have my friends talk about the random stuff going on in their lives, and it's nice to shift the focus to this conversation.

MEDICATION

I started taking antianxiety medications when I was sixteen. I take the selective serotonin reuptake inhibitor (SSRI) Zoloft, which I think is technically an antidepressant, but whatever it is, it's what was prescribed to me by my psychiatrist. I take a low dose, but it has definitely helped a lot.

I know a lot of parents aren't open to medications. My mom was like that a little bit, although I wouldn't say she was against it, but she did want me to try every other option first, and I don't think that's a bad thing. But if and when someone's anxiety gets really bad and is limiting or ruining their life experiences, I think that's probably worse than trying out a medication. Plenty of kids I know have found other ways, such as smoking weed or drinking, to try to deal with anxiety, so I guess you have to ask which is the better option.

I don't want to be dependent on medication forever, but I don't at all regret giving it a try; it's really helped, and I've had minimal side effects. Of course, how long I take it or how much of it I take is something I have to keep revisiting with my therapist and psychiatrist (who prescribes the meds).

HYPERFOCUS ON SOMETHING ELSE.

I know a lot of people who have anxiety will do sports or physical things that they can hyperfocus on, and this helps take away their anxiety a little bit. Well, for me . . . I hate sports, and I hate working out, so what I do is sing. Singing is something that I love so much, and it's one thing that can pull me out of any anxiety I'm experiencing. Since I can't just burst out in song, I make sure that there is always music on in every car I am in. My friends are all very used to my full-on concerts in the car.

The most important thing is that you want to find a passion not only that you love but also that is a kind of escape and something you can hyperfixate on—otherwise, it won't work as a distraction. For example, my emetophobia involves anxiety about eating for fear of getting sick, and I've found that watching TV while I eat can be a helpful distraction. If I'm with my family or friends when I'm eating, I don't watch TV since I can talk to them and that's a distraction, but when I'm alone, I watch TV so that I can basically forget about eating while I'm doing it. This might not be the healthiest solution, but for me, it would definitely be less healthy not to eat because I'm so anxious about what might happen afterward.

SOCIAL MEDIA

Social media isn't perfect, but I have found that if I'm feeling alone or like I'm the only person dealing with certain feelings or problems, I

DR. JUDY'S NOTES
STRATEGIES TO HELP MANAGE ANXIETY

f your teen struggles with anxiety, there is great news: it is a treatable and manageable condition, and we have many effective tools backed by scientific research to help.

There are many simple anxiety-management techniques you can share with your children and teens. They fall into four categories described below (a more detailed walk-through is available in my book *Stop Self-Sabotage*):

1. ***Thought modification.*** This involves managing the negative self-talk and worrisome thoughts that can take over your mind when you feel anxious. My favorite thought-modification technique is to examine the evidence. When a negative thought pops up in your head, ask yourself what evidence points to this thought being true and what evidence points to it being false. Almost always, you'll discover that most of your worrisome thoughts aren't unilaterally factual, which can help to reduce some stress.

2. ***Replacing troublesome thoughts.*** A great technique is "Yes . . . but," where you acknowledge something that is not so great about the situation but also recognize something that is more positive or shows work in progress. Here's an example: "Yes, I did not do well on my math test today, but I have been improving all semester, and I'll set aside more time to prepare for the next test."

3. ***De-emphasize the impact of negative thoughts.*** Sometimes it might feel difficult to use thought modification or replacement, or perhaps the thought is a reasonable worry to some extent (like being a bit anxious

about a big social event where you don't know many people). This is when trying to distance yourself from negative thoughts can be really helpful so they don't wreak havoc on your emotions and cause you to act in ways that might make the anxiety worse. One of my go-to tools is a strategy called labeling. First, identify a troublesome thought. Then, put this little phrase before that thought: "I am having the thought that . . ." For example, "I am having the thought that . . . I won't make any friends at this party." This makes that original thought a bit less scary because you are acknowledging that a thought is just a mental event. It is something you can observe happening rather than something that is absolutely true or defines you.

4. ***Reset the thermostat.*** Anxious thoughts and feelings can make you experience even more negative emotions or start to engage in avoidance behaviors to escape confronting your fears. The problem is, the more you avoid, the bigger anxiety can get in your mind. To counteract this, make sure you do something every day that brings you joy—I like to tell my clients to make a Joy List that includes all the things, big and small, that make them happy. Also, when you experience a troubling negative emotion, ask yourself, "What is the behavior or action I would take if I felt the opposite of how I do now?"—then do that thing. For example, if your emotion is fear, ask yourself what you would be doing if you felt brave, and then challenge yourself to do it.

Over time, you may notice that your teen can manage their anxiety well with these tools, and the anxiety is no longer something they fear! But if they need some extra support, that's OK too. (See the sidebar on page 64 for details on support options, such as professional therapy and treatment with medication, and how to choose the right mental health support person.)

know 100 percent that I can find people on social media who are dealing with the same issues. That's pretty much the best thing about social media. You can find people dealing with anxiety, depression, sexuality, and really whatever it is that you're trying to get through or struggling to understand.

What I've found is that a lot of people will share what they're dealing with and how they're coping. You might even discover a coping strategy that works for you, some seemingly silly thing that helps you feel better. When I was first dealing with emetophobia, I felt like I was so weird and that there was no way anyone else would understand the fears I was having, but I was wrong. I searched TikTok and found this whole community of people who are coping with the same anxieties. It was relieving and helpful to connect with others who understood. I'll talk more in future chapters about how to use social media in helpful ways.

WHEN ALL ELSE FAILS, CRY.

I don't cry out of sadness a lot, but I have cried as a way to help release feelings of anxiety. I know it sounds strange, but when I'm feeling overwhelmed by anxiety symptoms like lightheadedness or nausea, crying—like, *really* crying, even sobbing—helps make it go away.

HELPING SOMEONE WITH ANXIETY

I think the best way to respond to someone who is dealing with anxiety, whether it's your child or teen or your friend or sibling, is to be kind and understanding and to try to validate their feelings.

Obviously, I can only imagine what it's like not to know what to do when your child has anxiety or other mental health challenges. There's probably this panic of being unsure of what to say or how to comfort them. Maybe there's also some anger and frustration, too, because you don't know how to fix something for your child, and you just want it to go away (believe me, that's all your kids want too).

As a teen dealing with anxiety, I think the most important thing in a family is communication. That, and knowing my parents are willing to try to help me get through a challenging time. My parents have always been so supportive and helpful, but it wasn't like they just magically knew what to do. I know my mom talked to my therapist a little bit about what she could do or say to help me, and we've had to figure out together how to deal with it.

I remember once, I was driving my mom to our favorite local restaurant, which is just down the street from our house, and I just couldn't do it. I was hit by such extreme anxiety, and I started crying. My mom looked at me and realized it was very real for me. "OK, let's go home," she said. "I'm so sorry you're dealing with this. I don't know how to help you, but we'll figure it out together." This was probably the greatest thing she could have said. It made me feel loved and supported. It also helped me know that I wasn't alone, even if she didn't understand how I was feeling. I knew she didn't know what to do, but she was honest about it, and I knew that she truly wanted to help.

Going home or staying home isn't always the right answer. A lot of the time, my mom will ask me: "Do you *really* need to stay home? Because if you do, you can stay home. But are you going to have fun if you go?" Then, I start to think about it—and you know, my mom always seems to already know the answer, and she's always right, and if she pushes me a little bit, nudges me toward the decision of going, I often end up going, and then I have fun.

It's probably kind of a hard balance for parents—helping your kid decide whether they really have to stay home or if they can make it through. You want to help without giving anxiety all the control. Figuring that out takes so much communication, as well as being able to ask, "What do you need right now? Do you need comfort or a solution?"

"I wish my parents were more considerate of the things they say; snarky comments hurt."

—J., Colorado, seventeen

DR. JUDY'S NOTES

DEPRESSION AND ITS OVERLAP WITH ANXIETY— AND HOW TO GET HELP

Depression has become increasingly common among teens in the United States. This is especially the case for teen girls, who are almost three times as likely as teen boys to experience depressive symptoms. Thirteen percent of teens aged twelve to seventeen in America experienced at least one major depressive episode in the last year, compared with 8 percent about ten years prior. One in five teen girls—or nearly 2.4 million—have experienced at least one depressive episode in the past year, compared with 7 percent of teen boys.

There is a significant overlap between the experience of anxiety and depression. Oftentimes, teens will report that both are a concern for them. In fact, in one survey, seven out of ten US teens said that anxiety and depression are major problems among their peers. Anxiety and depression also share some common risk factors; for example, academic and social pressures tend to put teens at risk for experiencing both conditions.

Although practicing some self-taught coping techniques that are rooted in the scientific literature (see sidebar on page 60) is often helpful, sometimes your teen might need a bit of extra support from professionals to really experience symptom improvement. This is nothing to be ashamed about. There is still so much stigma about getting help, and if I could express one wish, it's that we would all support one another and understand that professionals are there to help people through these exact issues. No one needs to suffer alone when there are so many effective treatments. If you take some time to explore available services, you'll find something that works for your teen and fits their personality and preferences.

The most effective form of psychotherapy for anxiety and depression to date is cognitive-behavioral therapy. This is an evidence-based set of techniques that teaches people how to manage their thoughts, feelings, and behaviors by identifying triggers for anxiety and depression and learning coping strategies to deal with stressful moments and reduce symptoms in real time. This type of therapy is very hands-on, includes practical tips and guidance, and builds self-esteem and resilience in the face of challenges to help people feel more confident to tackle issues that come their way.

It may also be helpful to consider medication therapies with a medical provider who specializes in mental health concerns, such as a psychiatrist. Usually, the first-line medication strategy for managing anxiety and/or depression will involve an SSRI, which is a well-studied class of medication that helps to alter neurotransmitter function in the brain to achieve feelings of well-being and to increase calm and positive emotions. Be patient with the psychiatrist you choose; it will take a little while to find the best type of medication (there are many different types of SSRIs) and the optimal dose for your teen to feel their best. This can take somewhere between six weeks to a few months, but people generally report starting to feel better and experiencing some improvement within two to four weeks.

Going to a mental health provider for professional support is a very important and personal experience. It is crucial that you find a provider (or providers) your teen is comfortable with. Make sure you take the

NO ONE NEEDS TO SUFFER ALONE WHEN THERE ARE SO MANY EFFECTIVE TREATMENTS.

time to interview providers and ask them about their training, their experience with the types of concerns your teen has, and their initial ideas for treatment approaches and strategies for your teen. Take the time to ask questions and consider your options before committing to starting with a provider. And during the treatment process, if you're not happy with how things are going, make sure to speak up. Providers usually will be very open to discussing your concerns with you and adjusting the treatment plan so that both you and your teen feel good about their progress.

GOING TO A MENTAL HEALTH PROVIDER FOR PROFESSIONAL SUPPORT IS A VERY IMPORTANT AND PERSONAL EXPERIENCE.

Also, I think it's important for parents to remember that they don't have to be a therapist. It wasn't really my parents' job to figure out or fix my anxiety, and I'm so, so grateful they helped get me into therapy. Mental health experts exist for a reason, and sometimes the best way to help is to get your child help rather than to be the one trying to give it.

And one other thing—schools need to talk about anxiety and depression! I don't know why mental health is something that still feels kind of secretive, when so many kids my age and younger are dealing with anxiety and depression. We always have drug talks in school, but you know, many people start using drugs because of anxiety and depression. Maybe if we had seminars and conversations about mental health in schools, we would learn how to better cope as we enter the adult world. This is something that perhaps parents could push for in their kids' schools—everyone would benefit.

If you have a child who has anxiety, know that it is so hard to deal with, but it's not impossible. I've been doing a lot of work on my anxiety, and it still limits the things I want to do. But I'm making progress, and it's something I have to be patient with. I'd say to teens, "Whatever you do, don't let it just settle in and stay in your life forever. Talk about it and get help, and start trying to find what works for you."

WHAT PARENTS SHOULD KNOW

- Anxiety can totally alter and disrupt a child's life, making them **feel consumed** by panic, fear, and worry.
- **It's very real**, even if you can't see it, and it's very common these days—even if your child isn't dealing with it, one of their friends probably is.
- If your kid is struggling with anxiety, it's most important that you **listen** to them, **validate** what they are feeling, and offer **support**.
- **It's OK** if, as the parent, you really feel that you don't know how to help, even if you want to. There are a lot of **online resources** that will teach you and your teen strategies that can help. There is also **professional help**, and therapy specifically can be so helpful for anxiety and other mental health issues. Plus, a therapist can provide additional tools for both the person experiencing anxiety and their family members.
- Medication is not the worst option. The **actual worst option** is having a teen who suffers and struggles through life because of their anxiety. If your teen asks for prescription help and it's recommended by a therapist or doctor, it's important for parents to consider it.

SIGNS OF SUICIDAL THOUGHTS AND SELF-HARM

Suicide and self-harm are increasing public health problems among youth. Suicide is the second leading cause of death among adolescents aged fifteen to nineteen. Suicide attempts among black and Hispanic youth are almost two times higher than white youth, and LGBTQ+ youth are almost five times more likely to attempt suicide as their straight peers. Each year approximately one in five females and one in seven males harm themselves on purpose.

SUICIDE IS THE SECOND LEADING CAUSE OF DEATH AMONG ADOLESCENTS AGED FIFTEEN TO NINETEEN.

You don't have to be a professional to support your teen who might be experiencing self-harm or suicidal thoughts, and spotting warning signs is crucial to preventing youth self-harm and suicide. A number of stressful experiences can contribute to a teen's desire to self-harm or commit suicide, including loss of an important person through breakup or death, child abuse, severe bullying, intense pressure to achieve at school, or unmanaged depression or anxiety symptoms—so pay special attention to how your teen copes with these types of situations. Here are some of the most important signs of self-harm and suicidal thoughts to watch for in your teen:

- Talking or writing about death, dying, self-harm, or a wish to commit suicide and/or saying things like "I wish I wasn't here anymore," "What's the point of life," "There's no reason to live," "I wish I were dead," and/or "I wonder if anyone would miss me if I wasn't here"

- Expressing feelings of hopelessness and withdrawing from family and friends

- Giving away important possessions to family or friends

- Talking about being a burden to people and saying things like "Everyone would be better off if I were dead"

SPOTTING WARNING SIGNS IS CRUCIAL TO PREVENTING YOUTH SELF-HARM AND SUICIDE.

- Seeing signs of self-injury on your teen (cuts, scratches, burns, hitting themselves, banging self against hard objects)

- Increasing use of alcohol or drugs and/or doing dangerous things (like driving recklessly)

- Looking for access to guns, medications, or knives

- Significant and persistent change in mood

If you notice any of the above signs, talk to your teen right away. Listen and encourage them to talk; tell them how much you love them; acknowledge their feelings; provide reassurance that you are there to help; and seek professional help. This may include calling a help line, contacting a therapist, or calling 911 if your teen may be imminently at risk for a suicide attempt and staying with them physically until professional help arrives. To help your teen stay safe, you may need to take some significant measures, like making sure you know where they are when they're outside the home, checking up on them frequently, removing locks on their bedroom doors, and ensuring they don't have access to means for self-harm like knives, medicine cabinets, or firearms. There are several resources on page 167 where you and your teen can receive confidential support quickly.

EACH YEAR APPROXIMATELY ONE IN FIVE FEMALES AND ONE IN SEVEN MALES HARM THEMSELVES ON PURPOSE.

16 Hours

I have spent the last sixteen hours on my phone.

Out of twenty-four hours,

sixteen have been used for others

Who decided this device would help humankind?

It just messes with my mind

and creates unnecessary problems

My worth is now being determined

by how many people like my post

What is up with that?

I wish I could delete it,

but I can't for so many reasons

I have a box of radiation in my hand,

And instead of finding the joy in the world,

I'm annoyed that there is a picture of me on your page.

CHAPTER 3

SOCIAL MEDIA

A Box of Radiation in My Hand

Social media has become such a toxic place. And when I say social media, I'm talking about Instagram, TikTok, and Snapchat because, let's face it, if you're a teenager or a young person, you're not on Twitter or Facebook. (Of course, social media is always changing, so by tomorrow, there might be something new that every teen is using.)

The toxicity entangles a lot of teenagers, and all genders are affected, although perhaps in different ways because different groups tend to use social media differently. I know that personally, I've seen teenage girls and really just girls in general—including full-on adult women—get so caught up in jealousy about how other people look, their possessions, where they're traveling, et cetera. It's twisted that these totally filtered—even staged—images of other people's lives can make us feel that we want what they have so badly that we begin to dislike them. Yet it's such an incomplete picture! Who knows what else is going on outside the frame . . . and whether or not those people are *happy*.

Don't you want to just not care?! I try really hard not to care, but pretty much everyone knows by now that social media companies have designed these apps to pull us in deep. It's a struggle not to feel an emotional reaction to what you're seeing as you scroll. And it's even harder not to feel anything about how many likes you get or don't get.

BORN INTO THIS

As I'm writing this, I'm seventeen and a junior in high school, and I've been on social media for almost ten years at this point. I was around eight years old when I got a Snapchat account, and then just a little later, I got an Instagram account.

What this means is that most of the earliest memories of my life overlap with getting started with social media. I would guess that my experience is fairly typical and that most kids under age ten have no idea what life was like before social media. And we, those in my age group, 100 percent don't know what life was like before phones were everywhere.

"WELL, WHEN I WAS A KID . . ."

Parents and adults like to talk about how things weren't always this way. You'd call people on a house phone that was connected to the wall, have pictures printed from a film camera—and if you wanted to share these, you had to *mail* them. Life was so different when they were growing up.

Sometimes I wish that I could experience what things were like for older generations because it was all so different. That said, I'm so used to how things are now that, honestly, I can't even imagine the world operating any other way. So while I can agree with adults at dinner parties that phones are taking over the world and changing kids forever, I'm really just pretending like I knew a life before them.

A FORCED BREAK . . . THE BEST THING EVER?

When I was between the ages of ten and fifteen, I went to a two-week sleepaway camp each summer in the Sierra Mountains. We had no access to any electronics or devices. This meant no social media, no texting, and no contact with the outside world. I met my best friend, Laney, there. It was so refreshing to take a step back and enjoy nature and meet new people. Laney changed my life, and had I not gone to this camp, or had I met her somewhere else, I probably would have been too busy scrolling through Instagram to walk up and introduce myself to her.

While I am not the biggest fan of nature, it was great not to worry about what I looked like all the time or have to deal with any drama going on. Camp is like a bubble; everything stays inside, and nothing from the outside comes in. It is so important to take breaks from social media like this. The only downside is that when I came home at the end of the two weeks, I felt extremely out of the loop with my social life at home. I felt like people forgot me, and I was jealous that my friends could be perfectly happy without me. I later came to realize that none of that was true and that it was such a small part of my life—but that is a hard conclusion to come to when you are in the moment.

What parents seem to forget sometimes is the fact that when they were growing up, they didn't do anything to make their lives function in any certain way—it's just the way things were. And this is equally true for kids who are growing up in the twenty-first century—we are also just living our lives at a time when things are just the way they are; we have no control over that. I never asked for social media and phones to be such a big part of how we live, but here they are . . . and they're not going anywhere anytime soon.

The younger generations are even more hooked. I have watched my youngest sister, Coco, who is eleven, have playdates where they just straight-up sit on their phones the entire time. I have also watched Coco play Roblox for, like, twenty-two hours straight, her eyes peeled open and strained. Kids her age are being groomed to live practically their entire lives online.

Of course, they are also just growing up in a time where things are just the way they are. I don't know where it's all headed, but I often feel like life is too short to be spent this way. I could wish things were different all day long, but it would be a complete waste of time—this is the world we were born into.

NO ESCAPE

My mom will tell me stories of when she was a kid and how there'd be drama at school or something and she'd go home, and it would be like an escape from that drama. Maybe you'd even go home, and people would forget about that thing, and the next day, you wouldn't have to deal with it. That does not happen anymore! If you have drama, like someone calling you names or getting in fights about boys, there is no leaving that stuff at school. All that drama follows you home in that little box of your phone, and it extends the unpleasant reality from one physical place to another; it's a loop that goes on forever. You can never catch a break.

I know it seems like there's an easy solution: don't log on to social media . . . duh. Just don't check your phone! But that's just not a real solution. (To any adult or parent who thinks it should be easy, I would *politely* challenge them to stop checking their own social media

"I took a six-month break from all social media, and although my mental health was still bad, I realized I stopped comparing myself to others, and my self-image became more confident."
—M., California, seventeen

accounts or to stop text messaging—because that's a more comparable challenge.) All my friends have social media accounts, and for as long as I can remember, that's how we have contacted one another. If something funny happens at school, you're messaging in your next class about it. If plans are being made for the weekend, you're chatting about it online. You are literally left out of the conversation if you're not on social media. Basically, no social media = no social life. I wish I could say it's not how I stay connected to my friends, but it's truly the only way I do.

Unfortunately, it can also be how you are connected to people who are not your friends . . .

HOW A MIDDLE SCHOOL GROUP CHAT LANDED ME IN THE PRINCIPAL'S OFFICE

When I was in middle school, I had a pretty crappy experience that all started on social media. Most kids were using it regularly by then, and it quickly became a space where harassment was happening.

I didn't have a lot of friends at the time—girls can be such unkind b*tches to one another at this age that it's easy to develop a mutual dislike for each other—but I still had girls who would look out for me, as I would them. (I can't even begin to get into the complexities of the middle school girl world, but let's just say it's a strange time, loaded with a lot of internal and external drama.) We would send screenshots to each other of what people were saying about each other's Instagram posts, or whatever it might be, saying awful things. It was the way we gossiped about one another or kept tabs on who was saying stuff about us.

At one point, someone actually printed out, like, forty pages of screenshots from a group chat made up of some guys from my school. The chat was called "HM," which I found out stood for Hate Max. Nice, right? I mean, it's not even very creative, so whatever. Still, it's weird to

DR. JUDY'S NOTES
THE NEED FOR SOCIAL CONNECTION

Social connection, or the quality of relationships we have with others, is a fundamental human need; we are social beings. Research shows that a lack of social connection leads to all kinds of negative physical and mental health effects, including chronic illnesses; a higher risk for diabetes, pain disorders, and obesity; increased stress, anxiety, and hopelessness; and decreased feelings of overall well-being. When we feel lonely or bored or miss our loved ones, it's no wonder we would reach for social media for some of that much-needed connectedness—especially because it is so easily accessible and right at our fingertips.

The development of social skills is a fundamental process that is crucial in childhood and the teen years, and like it or not, we live in a digitally connected society, and therefore, some level of connection must occur in the online world. Ninety-two percent of adolescents aged thirteen to seventeen are online daily, with 73 percent using smartphones and 45 percent reporting social media usage of around two hours daily. Clearly, there are a lot of positive uses for social media, from helping youth make new friends to keeping up relationships with their existing ones. However, a third of teens agreed that using social media somewhat detracts from the time they could be spending

RESEARCH SHOWS THAT A LACK OF SOCIAL CONNECTION LEADS TO ALL KINDS OF NEGATIVE PHYSICAL AND MENTAL HEALTH EFFECTS

SOCIAL SKILLS BUILT ONLINE DON'T EASILY TRANSLATE TO IN-PERSON INTERACTIONS.

with people face to face, and 44 percent admitted that using social media takes away from quality interactions when they are with their friends in real life.

Further, social skills built online don't easily translate to in-person interactions. The screen-based nature of online communication can make it less risky or less uncomfortable for some to interact, but in real life, things happen simultaneously and quickly, requiring prosocial responses in the moment and the reading of body language to know how to appropriately respond next. If a teen already has preexisting social anxiety and negative self-judgments, these fears can be heightened during in-person interactions, which may cause them to isolate further into the online world, where much more superficial levels of social engagement occur at a higher frequency. These superficial conversations don't do much to fulfill our human need for real, quality connection, and they do not provide opportunities for practicing the real-life social skills development that youth need to be able to succeed in all aspects of life as they grow.

This is why it is vitally important for us all—adults and teens—to value our offline interactions and understand that online socializing is not a substitute for the very special and unique type of connection you get from in-real-life interactions. People tend to report enjoying their time with friends and family much more when they are not distracted by their devices and are singularly focused on quality time. It doesn't take much—even twenty minutes of dedicated time in person with someone special, without dealing with social media, can feel satisfying and increase feelings of belonging and connectedness.

Challenge yourself to have at least one quality in-person social interaction daily with an important person in your life, and give that person your undivided time and attention—it is the best and most inexpensive gift you can give someone to show them that you care. Plus, it gives you the opportunity to hone your social skills and improve your mood and well-being. Use this challenge to motivate your teen to follow suit—show them your undivided attention for twenty minutes a day, and ask them to pay it forward and give this wonderful gift to someone else they care about. Remember, you are one of the key role models in your teen's life, and if they see that you also practice what you preach, it will help them to take your guidance and advice seriously.

REMEMBER, YOU ARE ONE OF THE KEY ROLE MODELS IN YOUR TEEN'S LIFE, AND IF THEY SEE THAT YOU ALSO PRACTICE WHAT YOU PREACH, IT WILL HELP THEM TO TAKE YOUR GUIDANCE AND ADVICE SERIOUSLY.

find out something like this is happening—especially because I never really did anything to these guys. In the past, I had made a joke about how I was going to win the class president election because one of the guys forgot his slip to sign up or something, but it was a *joke*. It feels silly to even mention this detail, but it's worth sharing because it tells you how things can kind of spiral and grow so much bigger on social media . . . even when it starts out as something small.

So who were these HM guys? I was in theater with some of them; I had dated some of them . . . I seriously thought we were all chill. But then I found out they had this group, and they were talking about how they hated me and wanted me to get expelled, how they were going to go to the dean about me. Even though this was all taking place only on social media, it wasn't just going to go away once we were back in the halls of our school.

The day after I got the printed screenshots handed to me, I had to go into the principal's office with this group of guys. While it certainly felt like I was the one who was clearly being bullied in the situation, somehow, these guys said it was justified because they just didn't like me. It was confusing, as was the attempt at resolution. They all sat around me in a circle, with the principal sitting next to me, and they shared, face to face, all the things they hated about me, all the things that were wrong with me, and I had to sit there and basically apologize for all the

EVEN THOUGH THIS WAS ALL TAKING PLACE ONLY ON SOCIAL MEDIA, IT WASN'T JUST GOING TO GO AWAY ONCE WE WERE BACK IN THE HALLS OF OUR SCHOOL.

reasons they didn't like me. The principal didn't even say anything; he just sat there. It was so traumatizing, but my mom really helped me get through it by reminding me that middle school was not my entire life, and things would get better from here. She also said that most of the boys would be more annoyed if I didn't care about what they did, so I opted for not caring.

That wasn't the end of social media harassment for me. I've gotten terrible comments since . . . harassment via DMs, negative comments on my being bisexual or gay, how I'm going to hell. I don't know if I've just gotten used to it, but those don't really bother me as much as what happened in middle school. Maybe it was the newness of it all or the way it happened, but it really made me sad.

All this is to say that if you have a teen in middle school, know that cruelness exists at this age, and it may be shocking to you. You can help your teens rise above and survive it by (1) telling them not to lower themselves by engaging in harassment of others and (2) encouraging them to seek support from family or friends they can really trust. Even if they have friends who may just be temporary friends, if your kid has someone willing to stick up for them, who will tell them what's going on when it's happening behind their back, tell them to take all the support they can get throughout this challenging time in their life! It will get better.

ALL ABOUT THE NUMBERS

One of the unhealthiest parts of social media is the fixation with numbers—as in how many likes we get, how many followers we have, et cetera. It's unhealthy because so many people my age equate these numbers with their self-worth.

No one—kids, adults, anyone—should care about these numbers. The rare exception of someone who should maybe care about their likes and shares is the person for whom social media is a career, but even for those people, these numbers have nothing to do with who they are as a human being. They mean nothing, *and* the numbers obsession can be super detrimental to mental health.

The risk is that you can get really caught up in comparing yourself to others, and this doesn't lead anywhere positive—especially when you start paying attention to this stuff when you're really young and it kind of becomes a part of your value system. You can start thinking things like, "Hey, this girl has five hundred followers, and I only have two hundred—that means she's better than me." It's so silly when you think about it (but we don't really *think* about it—it's more of an emotional or feeling response). Yet the number of followers we have says nothing about who we are as people—if we're nice to others, if we have any cool talents or unique features, what accomplishments we've made. It's just a collection of clicks on a button in an app on a phone.

I call it silly, but really, it can become kind of twisted and truly mess with your sense of self. I have a lot of friends who, if they get a hundred fewer likes than they got on their last post or whatever, will freak out and start to talk about how they must look ugly in that picture. Getting through the misery of middle school and high

"Social media definitely gives a fake perception of life, but I feel if I don't use it, I'll miss out."

—C., Pennsylvania, fifteen

school is already super hard for girls, and then to add this extra layer of comparison based on numbers that we can't even control . . . it can really crush your self-confidence at a time when you need it more than anything.

Somehow, I've been lucky enough not to get extra worked up over likes and number of followers and all that type of stuff. This might be because my mom never made numbers a big goal or point of focus. When she was on *The Real Housewives*, she would periodically check the ratings or her Instagram likes. Even when she did, she never seemed to care about the numbers themselves and would explain as much to me. She never let it define her or bring down her self-confidence, and I think watching her do that encouraged me to do the same.

The numbers I *am* obsessed with are my grades. I totally base my self-worth and sense of accomplishment on my grades, and I have since I was eleven years old. This is an equally unhealthy fixation—and something I'll talk more about in later chapters.

THE BEAST OF UNREAL BEAUTY

Of course, the social media comparisons really only start with the numbers—things can get even more dark and damaging when it comes to how "beauty" is defined on social media. There are so many influencers online now who make themselves look so thin or gorgeous—through angles, filters, professional lighting, makeup, whatever—that it's impossible not to get it in your head when you're scrolling.

Because of what my parents do, I've seen a little more behind the scenes of TV and social media production, and I still fall victim to it. I can see an image and think, "Wow, that's super edited," yet still get

DR. JUDY'S NOTES

FOMO, SOCIAL COMPARISONS, AND THE DOPAMINE-HIT ADDICTION

Children and teens are particularly susceptible to experiencing fear of missing out (FOMO) by using social media. FOMO causes anxiety for youth when they realize they were left out of a social circle or not invited to an important event. Seeing posts of their friends having fun inherently brings feelings of rejection and resentment and can lead to lowered self-esteem, loss of belongingness, heightened anxiety, and negative self-talk. This is because oftentimes, people see their digital personas as an extension of their self-concept. People compare themselves to others on social media and use this information to decide on their own self-worth and personal value. This phenomenon is very closely tied to social media use and even addiction. In fact, FOMO is a predictor of both how frequently and actively teens use several social media platforms, especially in problematic ways that might signal the onset of addictive-type behaviors. Temporarily, teens may find that it relieves their anxiety to know what their friends are up to when they are not around, but once they acquire this knowledge, they can become obsessive in trying to figure out why and when they were excluded from an event, as well as repetitively checking social media accounts to

> **PEOPLE COMPARE THEMSELVES TO OTHERS ON SOCIAL MEDIA AND USE THIS INFORMATION TO DECIDE ON THEIR OWN SELF-WORTH AND PERSONAL VALUE.**

make sure they didn't miss anything important or that their friends weren't lying to them. Anxious teens experiencing FOMO are also more likely to engage in phubbing behavior (ignoring someone you're with to look at your phone—for example, checking social media while at an in-real-life social function and finding it hard to stop).

Getting texts, likes, and positive messages on social media can be incredibly rewarding. They evoke feelings of happiness and satisfaction and temporarily boost self-esteem, but these feelings are short lived, and soon enough, people are on the hunt for that next dopamine hit. Dopamine is an endogenous (made in your brain) neurotransmitter that is responsible for both feelings of reward and motivation, and so people will seek that next dopamine surge by persistently checking their social media, looking for that next great message from a friend or an uptick in likes to a recent post. Over time, this feedback loop can cause people to lose touch with other important activities throughout the day and lead to decreased sleep and an increase in feelings of anxiety and depression.

It's essential to find a way to break this negative cycle and help vulnerable children and teens to build self-esteem in ways that are more self-sustaining. Parents can educate their children to practice activities that bolster self-esteem, such as these:

1. **Three things.** Name three things you appreciate about yourself every morning. Say them out loud, tell a friend or loved one, or write them down in your journal. This helps you get in touch with your positive aspects and gets you in the habit of recognizing them and your own inherent value.

2. **Working on a skill.** Learning and developing a new skill is a great way to boost self-esteem. Pick a few activities you'd like to try, and dedicate fifteen to twenty minutes

each day to learning and practicing them for a couple of weeks. If you really like the activity, keep going! If you realize it's not for you, select another activity to develop and practice. The goal is to find a few different activities or skills that you feel really good about and to continue working on them.

Here's a quick tip you can share with your teen: the next time you want to compulsively check your social media, pause and take a deep breath. You can also encourage your children to distract themselves by doing something else entertaining for ten to fifteen minutes. Oftentimes, after this period of reset, that urge to check goes away, and you can focus more on meaningful ways of social connection that will lead to lasting positive feelings.

stuck thinking I want to look like that. Even when my logical brain can see that there's SO MUCH EDITING going on to make a video or image look a certain way, it doesn't matter—self-doubt and criticism creep in, and I find myself thinking, "Oh my g-d, I'm never going to be that pretty!" or "Ugh, I'll never look like that in a bathing suit." It's twisted.

It's also dangerous. We idolize these girls who are something like size negative four, and they look a certain way—maybe they have big lips, sometimes big eyebrows, sometimes small eyebrows, depending on the trends. Not many people actually look like that, and the people who do have often had some surgery (which, to each their own—I'm totally game for surgery). Yet even if influencers come out and tell us to our faces (through our phones, lol) that they don't really look like this in some sort of "brave" exposé, saying things like, "Look, I wear a lot of makeup—this is my real skin," and they've got freckles or pimples or imperfections, they're still pretty, and most of us will never be able to figure out how to do that with our makeup to make ourselves look like that. I can't stop myself from thinking these things and feeling in some way that I'm never going to look good enough.

Of course, it's not only on social media that we can have experiences that make us feel insecure. I remember when I was about ten years old, I decided to start taking ballet again. I had quit every sport because I just hated them, but I thought ballet was beautiful, so I wanted to give it another shot. I showed up to the class, and it was filled with all these tiny, skinny girls. I was probably the biggest girl; I wasn't even big or anything, but I was much broader than these other little girls. And I remember during the class, the dance teacher kept telling me, "Suck in! Suck in!" I was sucking my stomach in so hard, and again he says, "You have to suck in! You cannot let your stomach hang out like this!" I was mortified because I was sucking in as hard as I possibly could.

I think if my mom hadn't taught me for so long not to care what others think, this incident would have scarred me for a long time—instead of mostly just making me laugh. From a young age, my mom would always tell me that it doesn't matter what anyone thinks except yourself. She would say things like, "You don't want to compare yourself and base yourself off other people, because you are perfect in your own way, and so is everyone else." Or she'd say, "This is a short life. You want to be happy." Or something like that. I don't remember everything from my childhood verbatim, but I know that these types of messages were repeated so often that I understand them in my heart; they're a part of how I look at and interact with the world.

My mom has always been very confident in herself. Since she had spent a lot of time in the image-focused worlds of TV and acting, she

"I think too often we're caught up [in] capturing the perfect picture instead of truly living in the moment and enjoying it. We're too obsessed with having a façade, in my opinion."
—C., New Jersey, twenty-one

"Social media has set up unrealistic expectations for life and has created a jealous environment. All we see are the best parts of everyone's lives, so it's easy to draw comparisons between our reality and the inaccurate realities of those around us."

—Y., California, eighteen

had to be, but it's because she *taught* herself to be that way. And she's taught me and my siblings to be the same way. Not to think we're better than anyone else but to remember that we are unique and that the best thing we can be is fully ourselves. Trends come and go and looks change, but self-confidence and acceptance don't go out of style.

I think parents underestimate how important it is to hear these messages, even starting from when kids are super young. I have a lot of friends who have body dysmorphia and eating disorders, which I know are clinical issues, but even others have maybe less severe but still damaging hatred toward themselves or their bodies. This kind of hatred and criticism no doubt stems somewhat from the fact that their moms (dads do it, too, I'm sure, but I've seen it mostly in moms) would always talk about their own weight and looks and constantly compare themselves to other women: "Wow, she's so pretty. I wish I looked like her," or "I look so fat today in this dress. I need to work out. I need to diet. I need to stop eating."

When you hear this stuff all the time as you're growing up, it becomes ingrained that you have to stop eating to be skinny or to be pretty. And this is so false on so many levels, but of course, girls start to think it's true when they hear it all around them. In a different but similar way, a lot of boys have grown up thinking that they have to be super muscular to be cool or successful. These messages affect kids way more than you think. Especially if they've been hearing them since they were two years old.

In reality, these types of messages affect everyone probably more than we consciously realize. All it takes is for one of your friends or someone on social media to say something about how they need to diet to get you to start questioning your own body. I'll find myself thinking things like, "Wow, they're way skinnier than me—if they need to diet, what am I doing?" or "Why doesn't my waist look like that if I am following the same routine?"

I'm not immune to these kinds of thoughts just because I'm confident about who I am . . . and I honestly don't think anyone is. I think the goal is to be OK with feeling insecure and asking yourself questions without that morphing into self-hatred. You can compare yourself to other people, but you don't want to let it overtake your entire life and make it define your worth.

SOCIAL MEDIA ADDICTION

We all know our social media use is out of control. I'm addicted to it, and so is pretty much everyone else I know. Sure, I tried deleting Snapchat once, and it was actually refreshing, but it was just because I was in a fight with my friend, and I couldn't deal with it. But I got it back so fast because I was super bored. When we were in COVID-19 times and I was doing remote school, my only form of communication was pretty much Snapchat. Even now, if I don't have it, I literally have no one to talk to—no one's going to go out of their way to text.

So basically, I'm not here to save anyone from social media because I can't even do that for myself. If I could offer any insight, it would be what I would say to my little sisters, which is that you shouldn't base anything off what you see on social media. You should consider everything to be fake—as in, think of everything you see like you would a movie.

I also would offer a piece of advice to parents who think that restricting their kids from social media is the answer: the strictest parents make the sneakiest kids. As I know from my friends who have restrictions on their social media—first of all, there are a billion ways to get around that—it quite literally does nothing. It makes them mad for no reason, and it's honestly hypocritical because the parents are getting mad at the kid for being on their phone too much while they're looking at Twitter themselves. Plus, the more access you have to something, the less you want it.

"I get inspired and more motivated when I see other people I associate with succeed. It makes me realize we are all human and anything can happen if you put the work in. So if I see someone I know having fun, being more 'successful,' it shows me that it is possible at my age and the circumstances we live under. But if someone tends to compare themselves to others instead of comparing themselves to their previous self, then social media can be extremely deteriorating."

—S., California, seventeen

I think my parents have helped me navigate this space with as much sanity as possible.

They've never threatened to take it away or put screen-time restrictions on it. It's made me, first of all, work to manage it myself and, second of all, not feel a need to hide anything or be thinking things like, "Oh, I need to find someone's phone so that I can text someone." Trusting me and giving me freedom has made me feel that I can talk openly about things that are going on. When the middle school bullying incident happened, I told my parents right away. But if I had been a kid who was forbidden from using social media, I might have hidden that and felt more alone and isolated.

A SPACE TO UNITE

When social media was first introduced, it was supposed to keep college kids connected and help them see what events were happening on campus. And I think every other form of social media that's come since presents us an opportunity to connect in ways that we are not taking advantage of. We could literally connect with someone across the world for free at any point; we could have these amazing conversations that open doors and help us learn about how others live, how others achieve goals we're working toward. Yet somehow, a lot of the time, we use it to get jealous of people who live within the same ten-mile radius as us. It's kind of funny when you think about it.

WHAT PARENTS SHOULD KNOW

- Just like a lot of adults, teens can have complicated feelings about social media—while it's an essential way to stay connected, it's also often a source of **unhealthy comparison** and can lead to a warped sense of self-image and low self-confidence.
- Because it's how kids stay connected, it's **not realistic** to suggest that your child or teen avoid social media completely—they will be left out of invites and conversations that allow them to be a part of the social environment at school.
- It's important to make sure that teens have an understanding that what they see on social media **isn't real**—it's **staged**, **edited**, **produced**, et cetera. They will probably still feel jealous or compare themselves, but in the back of their minds, they'll remember that almost everything they're seeing is fake.
- Encourage and insist upon **in-person time** with friends. Nothing compares to this kind of time, and it can help balance out the tons of time we spend online scrolling, commenting, and chatting.
- Social media use can become an **addictive behavior** and create a lot of deep emotions, ranging from excitement to anxiety, resentment, and rejection. If you feel like your teen is getting tormented by social media a bit, you can suggest they try some of the activities for building self-esteem that Dr. Judy shared in this chapter.

SIGNS OF CYBERBULLYING

Cyberbullying (using the internet, cell phone, video game systems, or other technology to hurt or embarrass another person) is on the rise, especially as teens are using the internet for just about everything. In past years, 43 percent of teens have been victims of cyberbullying, while 18 percent of males and 16 percent of females report bullying others online. Here are some examples of cyberbullying:

- Sending vicious or threatening emails or texts intended to hurt someone's feelings
- Sharing explicit pictures or private messages with others without consent
- Starting nasty rumors online or via text message
- Tricking someone into revealing personal information and then sending it to others
- Taunting someone to hurt or kill themselves using online technology

Cyberbullying is especially concerning because it can be difficult to tell if this is happening to your teen and to what extent. With new technology comes new means for teens to bully other teens, and the rapid debut of new social media platforms can make it difficult for parents to keep up on where their teen might be subjected to cyberbullying. It can also be more damaging than in-person bullying—people tend to be meaner to others online than they are face to face; the behavior can go on 24-7, making teens feel they have no escape; and cruel messages about a person

CYBERBULLYING IS ON THE RISE, ESPECIALLY AS TEENS ARE USING THE INTERNET FOR JUST ABOUT EVERYTHING.

can be left online for weeks or longer for others to view. Here are some signs that your teen might be experiencing cyberbullying:

- Becoming upset or angry after being online or using their phone

- Disengaging from use of the internet or their phone and sudden withdrawal from social media

- Reluctance to leave the home and refusal to participate in family or social activities

- Sudden and persistent emotional changes, like sadness, increased crying, or heightened anxiety

- Unwillingness to discuss or share information about their online accounts and activity

- Complaints of physical ailments, difficulty sleeping, and changes in eating patterns

Your teen may feel too embarrassed to talk about cyberbullying, but if you notice one or more of these signs, take immediate steps to identify and respond to what is upsetting your teen. Approach the discussion with an empathic and supportive tone, ask questions, express your concerns, and ask how you can help. Page 168 has several resources that can help educate you and your teen on cyberbullying and what you can do to stop it.

CYBERBULLYING IS ESPECIALLY CONCERNING BECAUSE IT CAN BE DIFFICULT TO TELL IF THIS IS HAPPENING TO YOUR TEEN AND TO WHAT EXTENT.

thanks for being my
ride or die. love you
so much.
xoxo,
Laney

CHAPTER 4

FRIENDSHIPS

The Best and the Worst

When you are young, friendships are all over the place. They can be lifesavers, the most fun ever, a major distraction, and unnecessarily dramatic . . . all rolled into one. When you're in middle school especially, there can be a lot of drama and crying. At that time of your life, you're trying to figure out who you are, who your friends are, where you fit in this bubble world of middle school, which is pretty much your entire world. In high school, you've figured yourself out a little bit—you understand your personality more, the type of people you like, and so on. There can definitely still be drama, but you have started to mature, and you better understand how to handle certain situations.

As I'm entering my last year of high school, I can look back and see what I've learned about friendship during my school years. Most of the "lessons" have come with much emotion and have created a lot of highs and lows. Which I guess is to be expected since when you are young, you are learning how to connect to and be close with people, and that's not always pretty. It's not easy to learn about friendship for the first time, and I can imagine that as a parent, it must be so tough to watch your kids' friendships form and fall apart, and you may not always know how to respond (the answer is usually no, you should not get involved). All I can say is that I've been through it and survived, and I'm here to report back what I've learned.

BASIC GUIDELINES OF FRIENDSHIP

One of the most important things with kids and friendship is being open to letting your kid try a lot of different things so that they'll meet a bunch of new people. You never really know when someone awesome is going to come into your kid's life. They could connect with someone through school, a hobby or shared interest, or your neighborhood, or they might even hit it off with someone online through social media or playing video games. I have made some of my best friends through TikTok and Snapchat.

Or maybe they could meet their best friend at camp, like me, when they just randomly decide to walk up and say, "Hi." They could also get extra lucky and happen to bond with your best friend's daughter, the kid they always have to hang out with by default but, by some magic, they totally love.

When a friendship starts, it can be really exciting and fun. But I definitely want to get to know someone before I spill my heart out to them. Especially in high school, and in some cases even in middle

TEEN TALK

"In high school, most kids care too much and follow after popularity and some fake personalities to fit in."
—N., California, eighteen

school, you have to trust someone before you share any deep stuff—people can be fake and just want to hear your secrets so that they can share them with others. And I'm not just saying that because I'm jaded; I've learned from personal experience—a guy I was dating a while back told everyone about my bisexuality before I really understood it myself.

I think a lot of times we can tell when someone is going to become a friend. I'm a very intuitive person, so I feel like I know pretty quickly if I'm going to vibe with someone I meet. If I do, I still don't try to force a friendship, because if you force it, it probably means it's not meant to happen and is just going to be a waste of your time and their time. And the reality is, you don't want to waste time, because life is short. So talk to your teen about trusting their gut feeling about someone before they even put effort into a new friendship.

Some other "rules" (or really suggestions) you can offer your kids when they're establishing friendships follow.

SURROUND YOURSELF WITH PEOPLE WHO HAVE SIMILAR MORALS.

I make sure the people I spend time around are those who have the same values as me. For me, this means I don't hang out with people who are

- mean to or always talking down to others,
- constantly comparing themselves in an unhealthy way (everyone compares themselves in some way, but there's a difference when it's super negative and happens all the time), or
- only concerned about appearances.

I also want my friends to be people who respect my values. That doesn't mean we have to agree on everything, but we do have to be respectful toward one another when we disagree.

DON'T FOCUS ON THE "POPULAR" CROWD.

I think what most people come to find is that the "popular" kids not only hate each other but hate themselves. I'm generalizing, obviously, but connecting with someone because of their social status doesn't create the best foundation for friendship. It's better to find and connect with people who make you happy, because once you leave high school, none of the popularity stuff is going to matter at all. If your goal is just to be popular and you walk out of the halls of your high school for the last time having had the best four years of your life, you have peaked too soon. Plus, you're a kid—you want to have fun and be happy, and if your friendships happen because you're trying to fit in or doing stuff only to make other people like you, that's not fun. At all. That's called pretending.

BE YOURSELF.

The opposite of pretending, or being fake to fit in, is being true to yourself. When you're young, it can feel scary to be yourself because it seems like everyone else is being fake or at least being kind of the same so that they can fit in. But the reason they're fake is because they're afraid of rejection or of someone seeing their true self. If you can be brave enough to be *your* authentic self, perhaps that can open the door to others doing the same—and then everyone can be less fake, and let's face it—less boring—overall.

TEEN TALK

"Everyone's exclusive and fake regardless of how long you've known them."

—Z, California, nineteen

> *"One of the biggest challenges is people not valuing me, like friends not putting in effort to our relationship."*
>
> —*I., Tennessee, seventeen*

TREAT PEOPLE HOW YOU WANT TO BE TREATED.

Even though this is super cheesy, and I don't think it's realistic in a lot of ways because the nicest people can get treated like crap, I still think it's a good rule of thumb. Because even though you might not get treated as well as you treat others, people around you will recognize the way you treat others and start standing up for you. Basically, you'll still get the benefits of being a good person, even if it happens indirectly.

Also, what I've found is that people who don't treat others well, those who say mean things about others, are typically revealing their insecurities when they pick on something about you. That girl who said something about your nose? She hates her own nose. This means if you want to reveal your insecurities, go right ahead and talk crap about others, but everyone else can see what's really going on.

BE LOYAL, RESPECTFUL, AND TRUSTWORTHY.

This is a really important trio when it comes to friendships. When you're loyal to a friend, you don't ever talk bad about them to others, you stand up for them when they're not around, and you still hang out with them even if you get into a relationship or whatever.

When you're respectful, you listen to and honor your friend's boundaries, their physical and emotional limits, their mental health, and their relationships with other people.

When you're trustworthy, you are true to your word, and you keep secret the things your friend told you in confidence. Of course, trust is always a two-way street. If they break your trust, they should have to earn it back. You don't just restore it without any extra effort or proof that they're not going to break it again.

DR. JUDY'S NOTES
THE IMPORTANCE OF A SOCIAL NETWORK OF SUPPORT

Humans require social relationships to form our identity, learn how to get along with others, develop crucial skills, reach goals, and navigate an increasingly complex world. Social connection is a fundamental human need and refers to a sense of being cared for, supported, and belonging. It can be centered on feeling connected to school, family, friends, and other important people and organizations in your life. Teens who feel a strong social connection are more likely to do well in school and are up to two-thirds less likely to participate in risky health behaviors, have substance abuse problems, experience violence, and/or have significant mental health struggles.

To meet social-connectivity needs, teens are expanding their social circles through social media and networked technologies. As we saw in our last chapter, a staggering ninety-two percent of teens aged thirteen to seventeen go online daily, and almost half report daily use of social media, with an average of two hours a day. Fifty-seven percent of teens have met a new friend online through social media sites or by playing online video games. But digital technologies can sometimes lead to a disconnection between online and offline interactions, and some teens

> **SOCIAL CONNECTION IS A FUNDAMENTAL HUMAN NEED AND REFERS TO A SENSE OF BEING CARED FOR, SUPPORTED, AND BELONGING.**

recognize that their relationships that are mainly developed and fostered online seem to lack depth or quality.

Junior high and high school can be a very exciting but also nerve-racking time. A recent survey showed that 19 percent of high schoolers have been bullied at school, 37 percent have felt sad or hopeless, and 19 percent have seriously contemplated attempting suicide. And because research has shown that quality social connectivity can be protective against some of these problems, it is imperative that teens take a look at their social relationships and think about how they can develop a rich network of support.

One way to do this is to take a social network inventory of all the people you and your teen regularly interact with both online and offline. Here are some instructions for your teen: Draw a small circle on a piece of paper, then a medium-size circle around the small circle, and finally, a large circle that envelops both the medium and small circles. Write the names of people who are in your "inner circle" in the small circle. These are the people you trust the most and whom you feel you can confide in about anything. Then, write down the names of people who are in your "middle circle." These are people you enjoy spending time with regularly and with whom you have things in common; you may feel comfortable talking about casual topics with these people but may not choose to delve deeply into more personal matters. Finally, in the largest circle, write the names of people who are in your "outer circle." These are people you socialize with from time to time and are friendly with, but most of your interactions are pretty superficial, and you don't generally get into offline (i.e., in-real-life) one-on-one conversations with these individuals on a regular basis.

Once you've taken your social inventory, what are some patterns you notice? What part of your "circle" do you need to strengthen? Do you wish to have more people in your inner circle, or are you happy with the people you've named?

Here are some ways to improve the quality of your social relationships and take your social connectivity to the next level:

1. ***Consider joining student-led clubs at your school.*** These clubs can create a fun and safe environment for you to meet new friends with whom you have commonalities.
2. ***Look for opportunities to volunteer in the community.*** It feels really good to give back, and you will have the opportunity to meet some great teens and adults who are well connected in your local area and might have other great ideas for fun and meaningful activities for you to try.
3. ***Find a mentor.*** Mentors can be very helpful in offering guidance and advice, especially if you want a different perspective from your parents or your regular group of friends. Generally, mentors are a few steps ahead of you in life (a bit older and have more life experience) and can tell you how they navigated similar issues when they were your age.
4. ***Ask your parents to support your pursuit of extracurricular activities.*** Have a hobby or activity you're interested in trying? Talk to your parents about giving you opportunities or outlets to get involved.

With some time and patience, anyone can improve their social connectivity at any time. Take a regular inventory of your social network, and think creatively about ways to make this more enriching and fulfilling for you. The benefits are enormous—those in your social network can help you get through some of the stresses that you encounter regularly as a teen.

SEVEN SECRETS TO CREATING LOW-DRAMA FRIENDSHIPS

Even if you try to do everything right in how you make and maintain friendships, it is literally impossible to escape drama in the friend department as a school-aged kid. I seriously don't know anyone who hasn't dealt with it at some point during the ages of eight to eighteen. But there are things you can suggest to your teen that will hopefully at least minimize the drama.

1. TRY NOT TO TALK SH*T (ESPECIALLY IF YOU'RE IN MIDDLE SCHOOL).

I think one of the things in middle school is that everyone seems to be making fun of other people's appearance or interests. I don't know why, and anyone in middle school can attest to this, but everyone wants to and does talk sh*t. There's some strange, inevitable pull to it, but it is so stupid and only creates problems and drama no one needs to deal with. But if you're a middle schooler, I still think you can try your hardest not to do it.

One way to stop yourself from doing it is to try to keep in mind that 99 percent of the time, talking badly about someone is a reflection of your own insecurities. That means if you want to tell everyone, "Oh, I'm insecure about this," then, yeah, go ahead and say that mean thing about someone else.

The truth is, it's a lot easier said than done to not talk sh*t because it's really hard to escape it when everyone's doing it, and it feels so awkward not to engage. But the more rumors and rudeness that come out of your mouth or are messaged on

TRY TO KEEP IN MIND THAT 99 PERCENT OF THE TIME, TALKING BADLY ABOUT SOMEONE IS A REFLECTION OF YOUR OWN INSECURITIES.

I'VE ALSO BECOME REALLY GOOD AT CHANGING THE SUBJECT WHEN SOMEONE STARTS TALKING BADLY ABOUT ANOTHER PERSON.

your phone or posted on your social media about others, the more you'll get the same thing coming back at you. You don't want enemies in middle school—or high school, either, but middle school is when kids can really turn on you . . . even people you think are your friends.

I've learned some techniques for trying to stay out of talking sh*t. I usually just smile when someone talks badly about someone else, and I try to turn it back on them by asking something like, "Oh my God, really? How did that make you feel?"; "What do you think about that?"; or "I understand that from your perspective." This way, you don't really have to say anything bad, and you are sympathizing without necessarily agreeing; you're staying neutral.

I've also become really good at changing the subject when someone starts talking badly about another person. Maybe I'll bring up something unrelated that I have to say. Or maybe I'll pull out my phone and just even open TikTok and be like, "This video is so funny," even if it's not—I just use anything to create a distraction from the drama, and it's super effective.

2. NEVER PUT ANYTHING IN WRITING.

My mom has always told me not to put anything negative about someone else in writing. This means not in text, not in email, not on social media. If you *text* about it, that message is going to get to that other person, maybe not right away, but it will happen. If you send a text message saying something like, "Oh, so-and-so is being so annoying today," that's going to create a whole new cycle. It's a new fight.

If you're mad at someone, you should *talk* about it, either to the person directly or to someone else. You're allowed to and should discuss your problems verbally with other friends; you can talk to someone else about being mad, or sad, or angry with a friend. But you should discuss it, get over it, and then it's done.

3. REMEMBER THAT NOT EVERYONE'S THE SAME.

When dealing with friendships, there's no single formula that's going to work with every person because everyone is different. This means that something that works for you and your best friend might not work for you and another friend. It's not always obvious at first, but with each individual, you have to learn how to best communicate and work through things that come up. It's just part of the learning process with friendships.

Here's an example: If my best friend and I get in a fight, we'll take a second off and recuperate and then come back and talk about it. Or sometimes we'll just say, "Yeah, whatever. Let's just ignore it," and it will die down. That works for us. But for some of my other friends, that would not work. They may need more of a makeup effort. They might need to verbally argue with me in order to release their anger and get over the fight.

A major part of figuring out what works with each person is communication. They have to be able to say, "I'm super emotional, and after a fight, I usually need some time before I can talk to someone again." And you have to be able to say, "I want to talk through stuff immediately and get it over with!" Then, you two can meet somewhere in the middle. What's hard about this is that when you're young, you don't always understand yourself yet; you don't know your strengths and weaknesses or what makes you feel better or worse about something. But you can start paying attention because the more you understand yourself, the better your relationships will be.

It's also important to remember that you can have friends who are into different things. For example, I have specific friends I know would go out and shop for crystals with me, and they'd have fun doing that. Other friends would rather go to the beach or the mall instead. It's cool to have people with diverse interests in your life because you can learn from them and discover new things.

4. REALIZE THAT MIDDLE SCHOOL AND HIGH SCHOOL REPRESENT SMALL OR VERY SMALL POOLS OF PEOPLE.

When you're young, a lot of drama happens around having crushes on people and dating and relationships. Usually this is because someone kissed someone else's crush or started dating that person you broke up with a while ago, et cetera. But when you think about it, your class size is probably relatively small, and then from that number, there's the potential number of people you might like as friends, and then an even smaller number of people you could like as more than friends—the odds of you and your friends liking the same people over the course of a few years are high. So I think if a relationship ended on good terms and someone goes and kisses your ex or dates them or whatever, you shouldn't get mad at people for exploring things.

And listen, I'm not saying this is easy. It takes a certain maturity. There is a level of respect and understanding to be had before this happens. Maybe a conversation with your friend on how they would feel if you dated someone they'd dated. That said, they do not control your life, and you are able to make your own decisions. Now, if someone has hurt you or your friend in a relationship, that's a different scenario, and you should naturally want to stay away from that person. But unless that is the case, you want to think about whether or not it's really worth it to be mad at a friend for liking or dating someone you used to like or date.

5. AVOID UNHEALTHY COMPETITION.

Similarly, you can keep the drama low by managing other areas where competition can lead to problems. This can be with things like grades and test scores and anywhere any type of performance is involved.

When I was in middle school (and some in high school), I used to get in fights with friends about grades and test scores. We would just get into fights about who did better and who studied less and got the higher grade . . . frustrating comparison stuff that would get under our skin.

What I learned is that I definitely had to adopt a different approach, which is to just not talk about it. I don't ask anymore, not because I don't care but because I don't want to get stuck comparing myself to others. Someone is going to get mad when grades and test scores come up, even if it's not you, so what's the point in talking about it? It's better to shift your thinking to the things you can control, which are your performance, grades, and test scores. Focus on working toward your own accomplishments, not out-accomplishing everyone else. And appreciate that others' accomplishments don't belittle yours. They can do amazing things. It doesn't mean your achievements aren't amazing as well, and it doesn't take away from what you've done.

FOCUS ON WORKING TOWARD YOUR OWN ACCOMPLISHMENTS, NOT OUT-ACCOMPLISHING EVERYONE ELSE. AND APPRECIATE THAT OTHERS' ACCOMPLISHMENTS DON'T BELITTLE YOURS.

6. KNOW WHEN IT'S TIME TO TAKE A BREAK.

Sometimes even the best of friends need time apart. It doesn't mean you're not supposed to be friends or that something is wrong with your friendship. You might just need to take time for yourself at some point, and that's OK. Even if other people start talking about it, saying, "Oh yeah, I heard Max and what's-her-face aren't talking right now," you don't have to buy into it as being more dramatic than it is. Honestly, you might even go through a whole school year without being as close to someone who was your best friend the year before, only to come back and be super tight again the next year. That's how young friendships are sometimes, and that's fine. Maybe you or they needed to grow a different way or learn about something apart from you so that you could be better friends later. Whatever it might be, just remember that you're allowed to take space or give space when it's needed. It doesn't mean someone is a bad person or that you're a bad person.

"In some friendships, it's easy to get jealous of someone's family dynamic, which we may not have but want. And you compare without fully understanding each other's different situations."

—A

7. LISTEN TO YOUR PARENTS.

I used to get mad at my mom for telling me how to deal with my friends because a lot of the time, it would seem like her solutions weren't right for the current times. For example, we can't just "go dark" on social media to make an issue go away. But I did start to realize that she, and probably other parents, really do know a lot. Even if we think we know more than they do, they actually do know more because they've lived and been through different stages of life already.

That being said, parent advice doesn't always fit 100 percent because (a) things are different now than when they were growing up, and (b) they don't know everything—it's not like you become a parent and are granted access to some secret formula to friendships.

All I'm saying is that when you're dealing with any friend drama or something that could become drama, I think it's important to give your parents a shot at helping. They will definitely have a more mature perspective, and you can always listen to what they have to say and then apply it in your own way. It's like taking a modern approach to a timeless problem.

The more general advice my parents have given me around friendship has always been good. They've taught me (1) to be true to myself, and if someone else can't deal with that, they're not the right friend for me; (2) that everything happens for a reason, and if I'm not supposed to be in a friendship, that's just how it is, and it will show itself to me eventually; and (3) to respect myself first and be confident in who I am.

A NOTE TO PARENTS: DO NOT GET INVOLVED WITH YOUR KIDS' DRAMA.

I'd like to add a little caveat to the note about listening to your parents, and this might be a little more of a "listen up, parents": please, for the sake of your kids, do not get involved in your kids' drama. And by drama, I mean things like if a kid is talking bad behind your kid's back to another one of their friends, or their middle school boyfriend says something mean, or your kid didn't get invited to an event. Basically, if it's something that will not affect them after a week or so, do not get involved unless they ask you to. I say this for two reasons: first of all, it makes your child not be able to deal with their own problems—it's now you dealing with their problems and not giving them a chance to do their own problem-solving—and second, it's so embarrassing.

There are exceptions, obviously. Like I said, if your child asks for your intervention, then they likely really need it, because no kid wants their parent to get involved. If you feel compelled to get involved before your kid has mentioned it, ask them before you do anything at all. Don't text other parents or anyone until you've gotten their permission because they most often will probably say something like, "No. Oh my God, that'll make it a hundred times worse." If it's stupid kid drama, parent involvement usually makes the situation worse. So do not get involved unless your child asks you to.

I think it's easier to distinguish the bad problems in middle school because that's when something might be more obviously detrimental. For example, when I had a whole group of guys saying negative things about me on social media, it was obvious that my mom had to get involved.

> **BASICALLY, IF IT'S SOMETHING THAT WILL NOT AFFECT THEM AFTER A WEEK OR SO, DO NOT GET INVOLVED UNLESS THEY ASK YOU TO.**

Preteens and teens shouldn't have to resolve situations like that on their own. Another example would be hearing that your child is getting bullied—parent intervention is definitely needed.

DR. JUDY'S NOTES
DEVELOPING YOUR ONLINE SOCIAL CAPITAL

ocial connectivity is crucial for great physical and mental health. And improving your offline relationships isn't the only way to grow your (and your teen's) social capital.

Networking has clearly shifted online, especially for the younger generations, and there are many wonderful benefits to communicating this way. You and your teen can connect globally with people who share your interests and passions, greatly expanding your community. But it can be harder to feel a real connection to someone virtually, and sometimes what you see isn't what you get. This is something that teens are constantly grappling with, which leads them to sometimes feel that their social lives are not very satisfying.

> SOCIAL CONNECTIVITY IS CRUCIAL FOR GREAT PHYSICAL AND MENTAL HEALTH.

Research has shown that the development and maintenance of relationships online is very common, and online intimacy can increase well-being. With some attention and care, these relationships can be similar in meaning, intimacy, and stability in comparison to offline relationships.

Research also shows that there are positive effects on well-being related to online social interactions, including increased self-esteem, better mood, greater perceived social support and reduced loneliness, and lower risk of depression and anxiety. However, as discussed earlier in greater detail (see chapter 3), other studies have suggested that increased social media use actually increases feelings of loneliness and depression, along with other deleterious consequences. I believe this conflicting information has to do with how one approaches their online relationships. To get the most out of them, we have to find ways to improve the quality of these friendships instead of focusing on being friends with as many people as possible.

Here are some helpful tips you can share with your teens to help them enrich friendships that are mostly digital in nature. (They are also great tips for your own social media use!)

1. ***Choose a few digital platforms that you and your teen can really invest in and that you care about.*** It is helpful to focus your energies on interacting socially on just one or two platforms. Think about platforms where you won't be passively scrolling through others' posts and just automatically liking dozens of posts; choose those that allow you to be more active and engage in meaningful dialogue and conversations with other people who share your interests, ideas, and values.

2. ***Connect with kindness, curiosity, and authenticity.*** When reaching out to new people with whom you and your teen hope to develop friendships, approach them with these three characteristics, and you'll experience a higher rate of success with actually fostering meaningful connections. Try reaching out by offering a sincere compliment (perhaps about a recent post or some work they shared) and then asking a question that prompts a long-form response (rather than a question that the person can easily answer yes or no to). Be yourself—don't try to fake a persona that isn't part of you, because that's going to take you away from genuine, quality connections that are worth your time.

Max also has some great suggestions in her "Basic Guidelines of Friendship" on page 94 that can help you and your teen connect meaningfully with others.

3. ***Only connect with people who make you feel good about yourself—and feel free to block and disconnect from those who don't.*** Try to cultivate friendships that help you and your teen to grow as people, make you feel great about yourself, and inspire you to be your best. It can be really tempting to chase clout and want to engage with people who have tons of followers or those who seem to have it all going on from the outside. But resist the temptation to try to earn people's likes and respect purely because of what you perceive their social network to be. And if anyone starts being mean to you or bullying you, cut them off. Block them, unfollow them, and stop communicating with them. Remember, it is your choice whom you talk to or don't talk to online, so if they aren't adding anything positive to your life, move on.

4. ***Take the time to nurture your online relationships the way that you would nurture your offline relationships.*** There are ways to have meaningful and deep connections with people you socialize with in a primarily online setting—but you have to put in the work. Make it a point to check in with those who are important to you by asking them how their day was, remembering important activities and events in their lives, and spending time engaging them one on one. Talk about your common interests and hobbies, and make it a point to learn something new about them as your friendship grows. Think of creative ways to spend quality time together that involve real-time interactions, for example, having a friend on FaceTime while you watch the same movie together from different locations or taking a virtual exercise class together.

HOW TO IDENTIFY AND END A TOXIC FRIENDSHIP

When a teen (or an adult) becomes friends with a toxic person, that friendship will ultimately become toxic too. Those personality traits of theirs that you thought were so cool and funny and dark will eventually be turned toward you. There are certain things to watch out for when identifying a toxic friend. A toxic friend:

MAKES YOU FEEL BAD FOR THINGS YOU CAN'T CONTROL

If you have mental health issues or struggle with anything and your "friend" makes you feel bad about this, they're not good for you. The same goes for if they make fun of you for the things you enjoy and/ or have a passion for.

KEEPS YOU ISOLATED FROM EVERYONE ELSE

If someone wants to be your only friend, but they want to have other friends, watch out.

IS RUDE TO YOUR FACE

Toxic friends are usually very bluntly rude. Let's say you've made it a point that you really like this new thing that you bought, and you're wearing it, and they say something like, "That's so ugly." They're telling

TEEN TALK

"One of the biggest challenges with having friends as a teen is letting go of friendships that you have outgrown or that have become toxic due to 'history' you have with the person."
—J., Colorado, seventeen

you it's ugly even though you've expressed how much you like it—that's rude. I don't mean rude in a way that's detrimental; it's just not nice, and it's not the kind of thing you want a friend to say to you.

TALKS BAD ABOUT YOUR FAMILY TO YOU

That's messed up, and it shouldn't be tolerated. Period.

WEAPONIZES THINGS YOU TELL THEM

If you tell them something in private and then they go and use it every time you get in a fight, that's toxic.

If you identify that you're in a toxic friendship and you're ready to end it, you want to take the high road if at all possible because you don't really need to make an enemy. And the truth is, maybe you just enjoy hanging out with them instead of having a deeper, emotional connection, which is what feels toxic or harmful. So what you want to do is shift the friendship until it changes or ends, or whatever your ultimate goal may be. You can do this by starting to distance yourself without directly burning the bridge by talking crap about that person.

IF YOU IDENTIFY THAT YOU'RE IN A TOXIC FRIENDSHIP AND YOU'RE READY TO END IT, YOU WANT TO TAKE THE HIGH ROAD IF AT ALL POSSIBLE.

With some people, you might need to say, "I need a break. It's not really you; it's just this whole friendship is feeling unhealthy. and I'm part of it too, but we should just take a little break. I still love you . . ." and whatever else you need to add to make it not seem like it's totally about them. And then, unless they reach out again, it's going to fade out eventually. But they probably won't reach out, because toxic people don't want to go back to people who have said they've done something wrong.

On the flip side, there are those golden friendships that you never want to end, like you hope they'll go on until the very end of time. When you have this type of friendship, you just know it in your heart and soul. For most kids, the awareness of having scored this type of friendship might not sink in until late in middle school, but when it does sink in, you want to encourage your preteen or teen to cherish those friendships because, as you probably already know, they don't come around often. Here are some of my favorite things to do to really show my closest friends how much I love them.

PRACTICE KINDNESS AND THOUGHTFULNESS.

In other words, going out of your way to do things. My friends and I will go out of our way to pick up small gifts or tokens of appreciation for each other for no special occasion. If we see something that reminds us of someone, maybe we'll just take a picture of it and send it to them. Or we'll pick up little gifts for each other, something like food or a trinket. These are just small gestures, but they can make a person's day. It's keeping them in mind and doing nice things.

SHARE YOUR APPRECIATION.

Sometimes I'll have a picture of a friend, and I'll put it on my story or my private story on Snapchat. And I'll say, "This appreciation post is for my best friend, thank you for everything. I love you." Whatever it might be. And then sometimes I'll just text my friends out of nowhere and be like, "I love you." And they're like, "Oh, I love you too." Showing your appreciation for them is really important, however that is in your love language or whatever. But make sure they know they're valued.

CREATE A SHARED CALENDAR.

It's hard sometimes when you're young to make the time you want to maintain your best friendships. But the good thing is, your friends are usually in the same boat—they're all going through the same schoolwork, classes, sports, et cetera. They're dealing with the same stuff, so they get it. But one thing that I've found helpful is creating a shared friends schedule and putting stuff on there that maybe you're doing or not doing, or when you're free. This is helpful because spending time together is the most important thing, so if you both or all make an effort to create that time, it will only make your friendships stronger.

WHAT PARENTS SHOULD KNOW

- Friendships during middle school and high school, *especially* middle school, can be **fully loaded with drama**. There's a lot of identity development going on and assessment of who might be your real versus fake friends.
- It's almost impossible to avoid the drama, but encourage your teens to take the high road as much as possible. This means swaying your teen away from (1) making friendships based on popularity and (2) talking badly about other kids. It also means suggesting that issues with friends be worked through in **in-person talks** instead of through texts and direct messages.
- Give kids space to create and nurture **online friendships**. Some of my best friends have been made through TikTok and Snapchat.
- Unless your teen is being emotionally or physically harmed, it's best to **stay out of their friend/peer drama**. In most cases, parent involvement only makes the situation worse. If you feel you have to get involved, please, for the sake of your kid, ask them for their permission—don't leave them out of the decision.

DEALING WITH THE LOSS OF FRIENDSHIPS

Quality friendships are crucial for teens to feel good about themselves and learn lifelong social skills. Making new friends, feeling accepted by others, and having a rich social life are sources of excitement for teens, but it is also common for social relationships to shift during the teen years. Losing friends or social circles is an experience that all teens go through at some point. Losing one friend is painful, but it can be even more challenging when teens fall out with an entire group of friends. This can cause all kinds of negative emotions and may lead the teen to withdraw from usual activities, become irritable, or disengage from schoolwork.

Although the eventual loss of friendship is inevitable, it is hard to watch your teen go through these painful experiences. Here are some tips to help your teen cope with this common loss:

1. Have conversations with your teen about their friendships on a regular basis, and if you learn about a falling out, acknowledge how painful and difficult that is. Listen empathically and discuss coping strategies. If appropriate, share your own experiences of friendship loss, how you felt, and how you ultimately coped with the situation. Ask your teen to come up with ideas for coping, and assure them that as painful as this is, it will pass.

2. Often, your teen might not understand how the rift happened and may feel blindsided. To help them achieve closure, it's important to talk about what led to the breakup so they don't bottle up their feelings or hold negative, inaccurate beliefs about the situation. If the relationship is worth trying to save, help your teen role-play how to approach the conversation with their friend with an open mind, rehearse an apology (if one is warranted), or walk through other appropriate solutions so your teen feels confident with next steps.

3. Give them time to heal. Every teen processes friendship loss differently. There is no specific timeline for moving on—it can take days or a few months. Check in regularly, and be careful not to judge your teen's progress. Let them know you are available to talk or brainstorm coping strategies, but also give them space to work this out on their own. Ultimately, all relationships are learning experiences, and when your teen heals, they will take some important lessons with them.

Tue, Feb 23, 7:47 PM

i hate that i miss u

CHAPTER 5

DATING AND RELATIONSHIPS

Are Things Always This Awkward?

The only thing more awkward than dating when you're a preteen or teen is *talking* about dating when you're a preteen or teen. Yet it's precisely the talking about it that can help minimize the drama between parents and kids.

Before "talking" about it in this chapter, I just want to say that, obviously, I'm just one kid, and I only have my personal dating experience (and my friends' experiences as well) to go by, but I'd bet that a lot of what I've learned about dating is pretty universal to teens. I know this can be a super-sensitive topic, especially between parents and their kids. But let's face it—if you are a parent and your child is within or approaching the age range of twelve to eighteen, or you yourself are the kid, you cannot avoid this topic because it's going to come up (if it hasn't already!). So let's all just be OK with it being a little awkward for a bit.

A big thing with dating and kids is when it should be allowed. I think a lot of parents are apprehensive about when it should start, and they put an age restriction on it, say, somewhere around fourteen or fifteen. To me, a preset age restriction is not beneficial, because it's not based on the personality of the kid, and in some cases, it can backfire.

I went on my first date when I was in fourth grade and probably ten years old. I went to the movies with this boy and his dad (talk about awkward). Afterward, we went to get ice cream and hung out at his house for a bit. It was so silly, but I guess fun because it was something new.

I continued to go on a lot of dates in my lower school years. Again, they were all kind of silly. I didn't even kiss a single one of them ever. So it wasn't anything like adult dates—it was more like two young kids hanging out without their friends around and calling it a date. Still, there are a lot of reasons why I think it was smart of my parents to let me start dating at a young age.

IT ESTABLISHED AN OPENNESS ON THE TOPIC AND MADE IT LESS INTRIGUING.

Since I was allowed to start dating relatively young and it wasn't made out to be this big dramatic deal, I never felt like it was something that should be secretive or kept from my parents. It was just like, "Oh, this is another thing you can explore and experience as a young person." And that's a really cool gift to give your kid—this trust and freedom to see what it's like to be your own independent person, even when you're totally dependent.

When you're younger, you're also still home all the time or at least still chaperoned most of the time. There's generally a parent or adult or caretaker around you or nearby wherever you go. This is different from later years, when you might spend more time alone with friends or dating partners. If you had to pick the best time to let your kids start exploring dating for the first time, which would it be?

"I started dating at thirteen. It was frustrating that my parents never left us alone. I'm eighteen now and still figuring out how to hug my partner."

—C., El Salvador, eighteen

Now, I'm not saying this just because a parent wants to monitor the whole dating thing and keep kids out of trouble. Sure, that's part of it, but honestly, more so, it's that as the kid, you're given more support to learn and talk about dating. And because it's not yet loaded with tons of emotion and hormones, you learn about it at a time when it feels more comfortable to do so. It's still awkward, but it's more goofy awkward than emotional-angst awkward.

I know some parents go so far as not allowing their teens to date while they're still living at home, which definitely doesn't make any sense to me. If your kids are out of the house when they start dating, they can't talk to you and learn from you in the same way. If they're still at home, you can easily talk about first dates and help teach them how to navigate and handle relationships, how to spot red flags, and so on. Obviously, some parents might choose to give certain guidance, such as about sex, in later years . . . although no twelve-year-old is going to be worse off if they hear that they should always, no matter what, be respected by anyone they spend time with.

All I really know is that for me personally, the fact that my parents let me take the mystery out of dating when I was very young made it easier to talk about. It created a foundation that we could build on and has allowed me to talk, especially with my mom, about things openly. (I may not tell her *every-thing*, but I tell her way more than most of my friends tell their parents, and it has brought us closer.)

IF YOUR KIDS ARE OUT OF THE HOUSE WHEN THEY START DATING, THEY CAN'T TALK TO YOU AND LEARN FROM YOU IN THE SAME WAY.

"I haven't dated yet, and I'm nineteen. I'm still kinda scared to approach it with my parents."

—T. M. E.

I would also say that because they were less strict, I've never felt the need to try to get away with anything. Like I've said before, the strictest parents make the sneakiest kids. The kids who never dated in middle school or still don't get to date in high school end up being super—or at least more—let's say *indiscriminate* about the choices they make.

IT ALLOWED ME TO HAVE VALUABLE LEARNING EXPERIENCES.

Young dating is all about learning . . . learning what kind of people you like and don't like to spend time around, what to look out for, and what your sexual preference might be. You might discover characteristics you value most, and this can be something that helps guide you in other areas, such as how you select friends.

Part of the learning experience might be kissing someone for the first time, which, in my opinion, is a good thing—hear me out, parents. The friends I have who are eighteen and have never kissed someone have a sort of embarrassed panic about it now. And while I wouldn't say they're desperate, they are definitely rushed; they feel like they have to try to catch up to people who had their first kiss in eighth grade or whenever. It's now like a competition, and when you're competing, you're not always going to do something because it's what you want; you might just do it because you want to "win." That could include not making the best decisions, maybe even trying to get ahead of everyone else to make up for being behind before.

If instead, preteens or teens get to do it on their own time—with support and guidance—they're more likely to only do things they want to do, rather than things they feel pressured into.

DR. JUDY'S NOTES

WHY THE RUSH?
TAKING THINGS ON YOUR OWN TIMETABLE

Remember when you were a teen and you felt like everyone around you was dating or in an important relationship—and that you were late to the game or playing catch-up? Well, consider your teen's experience; they likely feel the same way and may experience a significant pressure to start dating when they see or hear about their friends doing the same. It is important to help normalize these feelings for your teen. While dating and experiences with romance are somewhat common in the teen years, they are not universal. Approximately 35 percent of teens have some experience with a romantic relationship (from casual dating to a more serious, monogamous partnership) between the ages of thirteen and seventeen. This means that approximately 65 percent of teens have never been in a romantic relationship of any kind. It might be helpful to share these statistics with your teen so that they don't feel like they are the odd one out. It is also helpful to reassure your teen that while some will start dating earlier than others, any age your teen decides to start dating at is normal. Your teen may prefer to start "dating" someone with whom they have only connected via texting or direct messaging, which is not uncommon these days. Relationships developed in

> **REASSURE YOUR TEEN THAT WHILE SOME WILL START DATING EARLIER THAN OTHERS, ANY AGE YOUR TEEN DECIDES TO START DATING AT IS NORMAL.**

this space may feel safer and can soften the blow of any rejection your teen might feel if someone isn't into them. But eventually, relationships will involve offline interaction, so it's important to balance virtual communication with connections in real life. This is a significant teaching moment with your teens—to help them understand that they need to develop both online and offline skills in their romantic pursuits.

No matter where or when your teen's dating life begins, reassure them that they do not ever have to feel peer pressured into dating when they're not ready or to date someone they're not into. Sometimes teens might think everyone else is sexually active, when that isn't the truth. As a result, they might feel tempted to rush into a physical relationship because they think everyone else is doing it. But research shows that only 55 percent of male and female teens have had sexual intercourse by the age of eighteen, which means that almost half of teens will not have had these experiences during this time. Remind your teen that dating and sex are rites of passage that most everyone will go through on their own timetable. Becoming emotionally and physically intimate with someone builds social skills and empathy and will help them develop emotional intelligence, but these gains can be lost if teens engage in something before they're ready. Remind them to take their time.

REMIND YOUR TEEN THAT DATING AND SEX ARE RITES OF PASSAGE THAT MOST EVERYONE WILL GO THROUGH ON THEIR OWN TIMETABLE.

Parents should understand that romantic interests are normal and healthy during adolescence—you only need to think back to your own adolescence to remember this.

While the thought of your own child in a romantic relationship can cause anxiety and stress, it's likely an inevitable reality you will have to accept, so it's best to try to open the lines of communication so that you and your teen can talk about personal values, realistic expectations, and dating safety. As teens venture into dating, a great topic to start having conversations about is creating healthy boundaries, which can be divided into three categories:

1. **Emotional:** When you decide to share personal information, how to communicate your need for closeness and space, what your emotional needs are, and how you want to be treated.
2. **Physical:** How you want to be shown affection; how much you want to be touched; and when it's appropriate and feels comfortable to kiss, hug, and have sex. What are your zero-tolerance boundaries that are not OK for your dating partner to cross?
3. **Digital:** Everything that is related to smartphones, computers, and social media. This includes whether you'd like communication with someone you're dating to take place by old-fashioned phone calls, text, social media posts, or emails. When is it OK to share your relationship status or pictures with friends online?

Let your teen know that it is up to them to decide what boundaries are right for them. Once they make a decision about a boundary, teach them to communicate it directly to their dating partner and ask that they respect the hard lines your teen has drawn. It's a good way for teens to hold on to their self-concept and self-respect as they try to navigate the complicated world of dating and find the right dating partners.

PARENTS SHOULD UNDERSTAND THAT ROMANTIC INTERESTS ARE NORMAL AND HEALTHY DURING ADOLESCENCE.

Most kids *and* parents would probably say they are not looking forward to talking about dating with one another. For parents, I'm sure it's loaded with so much emotion and maybe disbelief—it marks a certain point of independence that's likely kind of shocking. And no kid really wants to talk to their parent about dating or having crushes on people, and they 1,000 percent don't want to hear sex be described by a parent. Yet if it's not the parent who does the talking, they're going to discover all of this stuff from someone else or somewhere else. Hello, internet, TikTok, et cetera. In fact, they've probably already gotten some or a lot of info that is a bit confusing, so why not just jump in the deep end and get it over with?

As a teen who's been a preteen, I can share a little about what's been helpful (and not helpful) for me when it comes to parent talks on the topic of dating and relationships.

CONSIDER TALKING ABOUT STUFF EARLIER THAN YOU THINK YOU NEED TO.

It seems like every year, teens and kids are reaching certain milestones younger. They're starting social media younger, they're dating younger, and so on, which means parents need to consider talking to them earlier about these things. That's not to say you should tell them at age two, but it should definitely be that if they have a question, you answer. You don't dodge it, because that just leads to more confusion and searching for answers elsewhere.

TEEN TALK

"I'm fifteen, and if I want to go on a date, it has to be supervised, and my grades can't slip."

—C., Florida, fifteen

> *"I was fourteen when I started dating, and I was in the closet, so I hid it from my parents."*
>
> —O., Canada, eighteen

ANSWER ALL THEIR QUESTIONS.

My mom has always been willing to answer every question I've had, whether it's been about sexuality, sex, relationships, respect, consent, and so on, which is definitely one of the reasons why we're so close. I'm able to talk to her about those things, and that has really been helpful for me. And she doesn't make it weird. She's never said, "I don't know; look it up." She'll say, "Yeah, I've been there. I get it. Let me tell you and I'll explain it to you, and we'll talk about it and I'll tell you the resources for everything." For example, when I brought up the topic of sexuality, she told me stories about her experience with friends in the queer community and what she knows about sexuality as a whole, and she showed me resources to understand it more.

My mom is very nonchalant about these topics. If she were more anxious about or avoided these conversations, I would be so much less comfortable with my sexuality, my relationships, and talking about all of it with her. That's not to say she doesn't keep it serious when it needs to be, but it's just not secretive. We also have fun with it. I can talk about cute guys with my mom, tell her about the new girls I meet, and I have even talked to her about getting Tinder when I'm eighteen. (Sadly, as she knows, I'm literally getting it to make friends.)

TEACH AND PRACTICE CONSENT.

Consent isn't just about sex; it's about understanding how you should expect to be treated and how you should treat other people. So it's probably something that should be discussed earlier on in a child's life. In fact, I've seen some videos on TikTok that show how to teach consent by using something as simple as the act of brushing hair. The video that stood out was one that has the parents ask their kids for consent to brush their hair without just doing it. I thought this was such a simple, great way to show how consent should work.

REMIND THEM THAT BEING YOURSELF IS BEST.

As a kid, when you're beginning to have crushes and wanting to be liked or wanting attention, you start to experiment with how to get what you want. You might try on different clothes and makeup or take up new hobbies to try to get closer to someone you like. I think at times like this, a lot of parents want to say something to keep their kids from trying too hard or straying too far from who they are. They might try saying something like, "You want someone to like you just the way you are," which, as a teen, you're just going to totally ignore or find annoying. It's not that the message is wrong; it just isn't the most effective way for it to be delivered, and with preteens and teens, it's all about the delivery. I think most kids would respond better to something like, "Confidence is attractive. And if you're confident in yourself, they'll be attracted to you and to your confidence."

VALIDATE THEIR EMOTIONS . . . WITH A DASH OF PERSPECTIVE.

Back in chapter 1, I talked about how parents can offer some larger-world perspective to kids when it comes to school stress, but they have to do it in a way kids can relate to. The same goes for dating. When you're dating or in a relationship as a teen and something happens that's upsetting and emotional, what you definitely don't want to hear from a parent is that "none of this is going to matter," "you'll forget

TEEN TALK

"I'm fifteen, and if my mom found out I was talking to a boy, she would be so mad. She's too overprotective."
—G., South Carolina, fifteen

about it in two years," or "this will mean nothing to you when you're older." Even if teens know that a relationship might not be forever, it can still feel totally important in the moment, and saying things like this only invalidates their experience.

I think the more a parent kind of minimizes a kid's experience (even by accident), the more that kid is going to retreat a little bit or turn inward with their thoughts and emotions. They might be open to talking through something initially, but if a parent just totally shuts it down, it can push them away and possibly toward whatever they were emotional about in the first place—such as an unhealthy relationship or person in their lives.

I THINK IT ALSO HELPS TO BE ON YOUR TEEN'S SIDE. IF I'M MAD AT SOMEONE I'M DATING, I WANT MY MOM TO BE MAD WITH ME.

I don't envy parents in these types of situations because it's almost impossible to say the "right" thing. Obviously, the right thing varies based on the kid and the scenario, but in my experience, what has helped is having my parents, mostly my mom, understand and validate my feelings while also—maybe after the emotions have settled down a bit—adding a little reminder that I'll get through it and move on to bigger, better things. I think it also helps to be on your teen's side. If I'm mad at someone I'm dating, I want my mom to be mad with me. I want her to feel the same emotions as me so that we can eat ice cream together and cry or have a post-breakup shopping experience together.

REMEMBER THAT TRUST IS A TWO-WAY STREET.

I've mentioned this before, but it's worth pointing out again in the context of conversations with kids about dating and relationships. My parents have always given me their trust, which has made it so much easier for me to trust them when talking about relationships and dating. In a lot of ways, it's when you start talking about these things that trust really begins to build and develop.

DR. JUDY'S NOTES

HOW YOU CAN PARENT TODAY TO HELP YOUR TEEN HAVE HEALTHIER RELATIONSHIPS TOMORROW

According to attachment theory, first proposed by psychiatrist John Bowlby and psychologist Mary Ainsworth, the quality of bonding a person receives from caregivers (parents and other important adults) early in their life often determines how they relate to others and respond to intimacy throughout their life. This means that parents and guardians have the important task of shaping the health of a child's relationships with their family and others, not only while they are young but long into the future.

Attachment theory is focused on the bonds between people and was first described by Bowlby as a "lasting psychological connectedness between human beings." It is thought that primary caregivers who are available, consistent, and responsive to their child's needs are more likely to raise children who develop a sense of security about who they are and how the world works. These secure children are more likely to explore their environment, interact with others, and not experience excessive fear in new situations because they know that they always have a secure home base to return to for protection and shelter when needed.

> **PARENTS AND GUARDIANS HAVE THE IMPORTANT TASK OF SHAPING THE HEALTH OF A CHILD'S RELATIONSHIPS WITH THEIR FAMILY AND OTHERS, NOT ONLY WHILE THEY ARE YOUNG BUT LONG INTO THE FUTURE.**

Decades of research has shown that a secure relationship with your child is one of the most important pillars of effective and empathetic parenting. And attachment begins to be established the minute your child is born! In fact, most researchers believe that the early years (between birth and age three) are a vital time period to help your child develop a secure attachment pattern and reap the benefits for the rest of their life. Children who have secure attachment are less anxious, are more playful, and have fewer conflicts with their parents. They are happier, kinder, more socially adept, and more trusting of others, and they have better relationships with family members and friends. They also tend to do well in school, are physically healthier, exercise more autonomy and independence, and go on to have more fulfilling and healthy relationships as they get older.

Through a series of studies, Ainsworth identified three main attachment styles in infants—secure, anxious-preoccupied, and dismissive-avoidant. A fourth attachment style, fearful-avoidant, was later identified. Understanding the different attachment styles can help you to develop strategies to cultivate healthier, more secure attachments in your children. Here are the styles as they relate to teens:

1. **Secure:** Secure teens usually grow up in a supportive environment where parents are consistently responsive to their needs. Teens who are securely attached are generally comfortable with being open about themselves, asking for help, and allowing others to lean on them at an emotional level. They have a positive outlook on life, are comfortable with emotional closeness, and seek physical and/or emotional bonds with others without a lot of fear of being rejected or overwhelmed.

2. **Anxious-preoccupied:** Teens usually develop this form of attachment when their parents are or have been inconsistent with their responses to them when

they need something. At times, these parents exhibit nurturing, caring, and attentive behaviors. Other times, they can be cold, rejecting, or emotionally detached. As a

IT'S NOT TOO LATE TO HEAL ATTACHMENTS IN YOUR CHILDREN— OR YOURSELF—IF THEY AREN'T IDEAL.

result, children don't know what to expect. As they become teens, they may want a lot of connection within their relationships, sometimes to the point of being "clingy." They are aware of any slight changes in the relationship, which can significantly increase anxiety. Teens who have this attachment style need more validation and approval from their peers and adults than teens with the other attachment styles.

3. *Dismissive-avoidant:* Teens usually develop this attachment style when their primary caregivers are not responsive to their needs or outright reject their needs. As they grow up, they learn to pull away emotionally as a way to avoid feelings of rejection. They become uncomfortable with emotional openness and may even tell themselves they don't really need close relationships.

4. *Fearful-avoidant:* Teens who have developed this style may have been exposed to prolonged abuse and/or neglect. These children grow up to fear intimacy within their relationships but also fear not having close relationships in their lives. They often have a difficult time trusting others. As a result, they avoid being emotionally open with others as a way to protect themselves because they don't want to be hurt and rejected.

It's not too late to heal attachments in your children— or yourself—if they aren't ideal. Even older adults can make great strides in rebuilding healthier attachments later in life and pass that along to their children. Here are some tips to get started:

1. *Learn to understand your teen's unique cues.* Be responsive to your teen's verbal and nonverbal cues for help, and make sure they know they can get your attention when they want to talk to you or when they need support. Every person is different, so learn your teen's cues for help, whether it's crying, isolating themselves, or acting annoyed. Let them know that you've noticed the changes in their behavior, and ask them how you can help.

2. *Communicate clearly and consistently to your teen about where you are and how you are feeling (and if it's a negative feeling, what you are doing to manage or cope with it).* It's helpful for your teen to know that you can be depended upon and are predictable. Let them know where you'll be if they need you, and if you're having a great or tough day, let them know that too. Healthy emotional expression (and healthy coping) can be modeled, and if they know you're having a hard day (and therefore are a bit more irritable or less attentive), telling them directly will help them to know that this isn't about them.

3. *Mind your own attachment style and how it interacts with your teen's.* If you grew up with an anxious-preoccupied attachment style, you may be more nervous when your teen becomes increasingly independent. Or if you grew up with a dismissive-avoidant attachment style, you may find yourself annoyed with a teen who might seem to have more emotional needs than you. Try your best to strike a balance and aim for the healthy interdependence that securely attached individuals have. Challenge yourself to get out of your comfort zone, and work to be attuned to what your teen needs at a given moment, even if you find yourself having some internal reactions or judgments.

I've learned a lot over the last seven years or so about navigating dating, and I think it'll help me have healthy relationships going forward. From what I can tell, healthy relationships consist of communication, respect, and an understanding that you don't need to have the same views on everything to be good for each other. I can break what I've learned about dating into five lessons—parents, you can pass this info on to your teens.

DATING WHEN YOU ARE YOUNG IS SUPPOSED TO BE FUN.

It's supposed to be a learning experience, really. Have fun, learn about people, learn how to spend time together, have conversations, go places together. If it's not fun or you're not being treated well, don't even waste any more of your time dating or hanging out with this person. Seriously. Don't do it. Get away, go back to your friends, go deep into a hobby, whatever it is you need to pull away from a negative person or pattern.

KEEP PERSPECTIVE, AND MAKE SURE YOU DON'T MAKE IT EVERYTHING.

IF IT'S NOT FUN OR YOU'RE NOT BEING TREATED WELL, DON'T EVEN WASTE ANY MORE OF YOUR TIME DATING OR HANGING OUT WITH THIS PERSON.

If you totally get swallowed up in a relationship, you'll miss out on your high school years and other types of learning about yourself at this time in your life . . . the big things like what you want to do with the rest of your life. People can get very wrapped up in their relationships and slowly start to be distanced from their friends. Friends will always be there, but people you date come and go. Always prioritize your friends who love you and have always been there for you. Romantic relationships really should be such a small part of your childhood—remember, you are still a kid!

I get that there are some people who marry their high school sweethearts, and I love that, but besides those people, relationships in high school are, a majority of the time, just a relationship and a temporary bond. You're probably not going to get married, and you're probably going to break up before college. Whatever you do, do *not* pick a college because of someone you are dating in high school.

KEEP AN OPEN MIND.

If you're in a relationship and you're closed minded and just think you're perfect and are not willing to learn anything at this age, then what's the point? It's valuable to learn how to be in a relationship with different types of people and to learn about their thoughts, feelings, and worldview—while also staying true to yourself. Because the point is to learn and to have fun. And if you are going in just to have the label or the social media presence, don't do it, because you won't grow at all—with or without that person, you're not going to grow.

DON'T TRY TO BE SOMEONE ELSE.

I know this is a little close to the "just the way you are" line I warned parents about earlier, but this is something I've had to learn through experience, so I'd like to share it. You want someone to like you for you and not who you're training yourself to be so that they like you. If you try to change yourself for someone else, they will not respect you. And if they don't want you the first time, don't pine for them or chase after them, because then they will *definitely* not respect you.

COMMUNICATE.

I think communication is the most important thing in any relationship ever, whether it's with your family, your friends, or someone you're dating. Communication is always key because it can solve a lot of problems and, even better, also prevent problems before they happen!

Having an open line of communication in every relationship creates trust and doesn't force you to try to read someone's mind or have them read yours. I also believe in being blunt and straightforward because there is no point in dancing around things when they're true. You also don't want to assume someone can pick up on all your hints when you're upset about something—hints do nothing, and they actually kind of undermine your point later because usually, the other person will feel kind of annoyed by the way the message was delivered.

> YOU ALSO DON'T WANT TO ASSUME SOMEONE CAN PICK UP ON ALL YOUR HINTS WHEN YOU'RE UPSET ABOUT SOMETHING.

What's cool is that even if you are not a good communicator, communicating that point alone can make you a good communicator, if that makes sense. It can help build your self-confidence just to state

TEEN TALK

"It's frustrating to not be able to hang out with someone of the opposite sex just because of assumptions."
—J., Colorado, seventeen

DR. JUDY'S NOTES
HOW TO HAVE BETTER RELATIONSHIPS AS A TEEN

If you want more fulfilling and exciting relationships in all the areas of your life (including dating), it's important to spend some time cultivating relationship skills and tools that will benefit you for years to come. Dating and building relationships of any kind take some work and self-reflection; but investing the time and effort will make relationships most enjoyable for you. Here are my top-five tips on how to experience healthier, happier relationships:

1. **Look at your patterns in important relationships.** Reflect on what your relationships have been like with your parents and other important adults. Think about any past romantic relationships or close friendships, what the strengths were, and where they went wrong (if this applies). When do you feel happiest or the most understood? Whom do you get along with most, and why? Do you tend to write people off if they've made one mistake, or do you give them way too many chances even if they haven't treated you well? Knowing your default pattern is the first step in changing any patterns that might prevent you from having great relationships.

2. **Don't look for someone to complete you.** A lot of these rom-coms really did us all a disservice. Learn ways to self-regulate and self-soothe instead of always looking to others to solve your problems. Practice being independent and relying on yourself in some areas, but also know that with other things, it is helpful to depend on people you trust. Remember, secure

attachment (which is a great goal for all of us) is knowing how to balance being independent and also relying on others without the fear that they'll abandon you or feeling the need to push people away to protect yourself.

DATING AND BUILDING RELATIONSHIPS OF ANY KIND TAKE SOME WORK AND SELF-REFLECTION; BUT INVESTING THE TIME AND EFFORT WILL MAKE RELATIONSHIPS MOST ENJOYABLE FOR YOU.

3. *Get out of your comfort zone.* Once you notice what your patterns are in relationships, practice doing the things you fear or dislike to achieve that balance that securely attached people have. If you tend to shy away from intimacy, push yourself a little to lean into closeness in relationships. If you are on the needy side, explore your own hobbies and interests and embrace your independence. The goal is to experience healthy interdependence—this means that you are flexible and can be independent when it is most appropriate or needed, but you also like depending on trusted others for support and being there to support others when they need you.

4. *Don't react emotionally—take a beat.* Dating relationships can really trigger our deepest insecurities. Sometimes, anything someone else does can set us off or feel like a personal attack, but oftentimes, these actions by others are less about you and a lot more about them and their own hang-ups. Before you are tempted to act on an emotional urge, take a deep breath and consider the pros and cons of doing something in that moment versus waiting a bit until cooler heads prevail. Talk to people you trust and ask them

to weigh in; sometimes it can be really helpful to get a trusted friend's perspective.

5. ***Create secure and healthy relationships in all the areas of your life.*** Decide what qualities are must-haves in your important relationships. List these qualities out in your journal or on a piece of paper to remind yourself of what's most important to you. Look to others who have relationships that you admire, and if you're comfortable, ask them how they were able to get to where they are in their dating lives. Most of all, don't settle for any relationship, friendship or otherwise, with people who might push you to violate your boundaries or values. Peer pressure can really suck, but don't allow yourself to be talked into a relationship that you really don't feel valued in and that doesn't bring out the best in you.

> MOST OF ALL, DON'T SETTLE FOR ANY RELATIONSHIP, FRIENDSHIP OR OTHERWISE, WITH PEOPLE WHO MIGHT PUSH YOU TO VIOLATE YOUR BOUNDARIES OR VALUES.

TOP-FIVE TIPS RECAP:
1. LOOK AT YOUR PATTERNS IN IMPORTANT RELATIONSHIPS.
2. DON'T LOOK FOR SOMEONE TO COMPLETE YOU.
3. GET OUT OF YOUR COMFORT ZONE.
4. DON'T REACT EMOTIONALLY—TAKE A BEAT.
5. CREATE SECURE AND HEALTHY RELATIONSHIPS IN ALL THE AREAS OF YOUR LIFE.

how you are, to say something like, "I'm not that comfortable with communication, but I'll try my best." You can also just say you'd prefer to text certain things because that's what you're comfortable with, at least to get a conversation started.

Try not to use a third party as a mediator, unless that person is part of your relationship. It's between the people involved in the relationship, and that's it.

WHAT PARENTS SHOULD KNOW

- Consider letting your preteen or teen date younger than you might initially be comfortable with. **Young dating** is usually super innocent, and it lets your kid get accustomed to interactions with others and, more importantly, makes dating seem less mysterious and exciting.
- **Talk about the big stuff**—dating, sex, consent, et cetera—earlier than you think you need to. Between social media and the internet, teens and kids can find info about anything they want. Wouldn't you rather be their first source of information?
- Establish **two-way trust** by allowing your kid to ask questions and giving them honest answers. Also, start off by trusting your kid rather than making them earn your trust. In other words, give them a clean slate at the beginning.
- **Teach confidence and healthy self-esteem** as much as possible. When teens feel like they deserve to be treated well, they're less likely to tolerate being treated poorly (i.e., less likely to end up in unhealthy relationships).

PINK FLAGS IN DATING, SUBTLE (AND NOT-SO-SUBTLE) SIGNS OF ABUSE

You may have heard of red flags in relationships that point to patterns of physical, sexual, or emotional abuse. As your teen navigates dating, there may be some zero-tolerance behaviors you've already discussed with them, like it's never OK if their partner hits them or forces them to do something sexually that they are not ready for. (If you haven't had that conversation yet, don't wait!) There are also subtler pink flags for dating, which signal a tendency toward abusive behaviors. These are signs that the relationship is likely heading in an overtly abusive direction, often signal some type of emotional or social control or micro-aggression, and should prompt your teen to consider stopping the relationship.

Share these pink flags of abuse with your teen:

- Catching their partner in repeated lies, even over nonconsequential things
- Keeping tabs on where your teen goes, monitoring their activity throughout the day, and demanding to know where they were at certain times
- Exerting control over how your teen dresses, who they hang out with, what they eat, and what activities they can participate in
- Isolating your teen from their support system and talking about their close friends and family in negative ways
- Not introducing your teen to their friends and making excuses for why that can't happen
- Periods of complete noncommunicativeness and refusal to answer questions about why they don't keep in touch between dates
- Unwillingness to engage in deeper conversations or to apologize when they misbehave
- Gaslighting and blaming your teen for things they didn't do
- Name-calling and putting your teen down
- Making jealous accusations when your teen hasn't done anything questionable

If you discover that your teen is in a relationship with several pink flags or one with red flags of overt abuse, you can share the resources on page 169 with your teen.

RHOC Alum Heather Dubrow's Daughter Max, 16, Comes Out as Bisexual: 'I Love You My Amazing Child'

"Always knew I was bi," Maximillia Dubrow

Dad
Jun 29, 2020, 11:57 PM

Let's take some time out tomorrow to have an awkward conversation

SHUT UP

I love you so much

i love you too ahha but never try to bring it up or i will kill you

Ok good to know. I don't want to die

didn't think so

Why would I bring it up? None of my business. Just be happy

CHAPTER 6

SEXUALITY

We Don't All Fit in the Same Story

When you're a kid, it can feel like the only life story that's possible is one where a man and a woman get married and have kids. Even though that's not the reality, it's the majority, and unless you come from a family with a different makeup or seek out different stories, it's sort of like, *this is it.*

But for kids who don't or won't fit that heteronormative mold, it can feel really isolating and confusing. Or, as in my case, it can just make you feel this awkward, intense sort of shock when you discover that there are other options, that sexuality isn't just male + female, the end.

It's not like I grew up or am growing up at a time where there aren't different sexualities represented in pop culture. But just because an adult understands that someone is gay or bisexual and knows what that means doesn't mean a child gets it. And I'm not talking about the sex part of things but the sexuality part. As a kid, you start to hear about crushes and such as early as kindergarten. You already know and hear about Lucas liking Layla, or whoever, and the excitement your friends have around all of that. Even for kids who are straight, the introduction of this kind of stuff can be confusing. Add to that a sort of absence of feeling around crushes on the opposite sex, and you can feel a little left out even early on. Maybe there should be some kind of pre–"birds and the bees" talk parents feel they have to give, just something like, "You know, it's not just boys can like girls, and vice versa. Sometimes boys like boys and girls like girls, and that's OK too." And this is a conversation that should be had with *all* kids, even those who will go the majority direction. That way, everyone will grow up knowing that people can have different preferences, and they will hopefully be more accepting of those who are different from them.

Introducing this idea isn't going to steer a kid in one direction over another; if someone is queer, they will find the path that takes them there. It's just helping a kid begin to think about who they are in a way that's supported and not secretive, and these are things that can help them feel more confident and accepted. It's really, really hard to be a preteen and super complicated to be a teen—if parents can do anything to help kids enter those years with even the slightest understanding that their story doesn't have to lead to that mainstream conclusion, they would be helping them in a major way.

THE DAY MY LIFE CHANGED

Like most people, I started high school at a school that was new to me. It was a private Catholic school in Orange County, California. Both of these places—the school and Orange County—were pretty conservative, but I didn't really have a lot of outside perspective since the latter had been my "home" since I was little.

It's weird to start a new school. You spend a lot of time trying to assess your new, older classmates and figure out whom you may know from your previous school. In my case, most of the kids had gone to middle school together, but I hadn't, so I didn't really have any carry-over friends (except for my twin brother). I remember, on my second day of high school, seeing this kid I've known my entire life and feeling

> *"I wish my parents understood that sexuality is not a choice, and it's not a trend or something we do for attention."*
>
> *—L.G.*

relieved that I could go talk to him. When I walked up to him, he was talking to the most gorgeous girl ever. (I'm not saying that because I was attracted to her, but I remember thinking she was just so pretty.) She introduced herself, and then we all kind of started talking, and then she ended up walking away.

When my friend turned back to me, he said, "Oh—she had to run and meet up with her girlfriend." I remember it vividly, and I remember thinking that people use the word *girlfriend* to describe a friend, but it just seemed different. I said, "Wait, you mean her *girlfriend*?"

And he said, "Oh, yes. She's bisexual. She's bi."

To which I responded, "What?"

"She's bisexual, you know—she likes girls and guys."

This may seem like a silly, small conversation, but it was literally the first time I had ever realized that being bisexual was an option. While I'm sure I had heard the term before, my world was really sheltered, and I think it took that real-life moment for me to understand its meaning and grasp it as an actual possibility.

This girl, I'll call her Rachel, ended up becoming my best friend at the time. She was a sophomore at the school while I was a freshman, and getting to know her changed my life. I had never questioned my sexuality before meeting her and understanding more about her life. She shared with me what she was going through and who she was dating and what it was like. She shared her experience of coming out to her family. It was so helpful—and actually inspiring—to meet someone who just really knew who she was. She called herself my lesbian guru because I would ask her all these questions. It can be so hard to distinguish your sexuality and feel like such a confusing time—having someone to talk to is a huge help.

I did end up having a major crush on her, but I never told her. Not because I wanted to keep it secret, but because I didn't really get what it was at the time. I knew it was a different feeling than I felt with most girls—or really anyone I had ever met before. But it wasn't something I could distinguish because I didn't understand it yet.

When I first was getting to know her, I was surprised that she was so open about her sexuality (I later found out that she wasn't out to teachers and staff) on her social media. Like I said, our school was really religious and conservative. Eventually, someone outed her to a teacher, and she ended up having to leave the school (they prevented her from participating in a lot of the activities she was interested in, so she left). She had been on a retreat with some other students when it came out that she was gay, and they made her sleep in a different room than the other girls. It was really messed up, and it revealed a lot about the school.

After she left the school, I kind of pushed off my questioning of my sexuality for a little bit. But then I dated this guy who was a complete jerk, and I just kept coming back to my thoughts and feelings about girls and maybe being bi. I started talking more about it and put myself out there. I told people I was questioning and trying to figure it out. I was never scared about what my school would think about my sexuality because I knew that if worse came to worst, it would make a great college essay.

I confided in the guy (the same jerk) I was dating about my sexuality and my confusion. Once I kinda decided I was bisexual, I told him, and he was pretty accepting. I later found out that he had told all of his friends and family about my sexuality before I even had a chance to fully figure it out. This was a complete invasion of privacy and should

DR. JUDY'S NOTES

SCIENCE REGARDING SEXUAL FLUIDITY

For some people, the individuals they are attracted to and their self-identified sexual orientation are fixed, like a characteristic or trait that doesn't change. But for others, their sexual orientation and the individuals they desire can fluctuate throughout their lives. These individuals might describe themselves as being sexually fluid. Questioning your sexuality can happen at any age. And this fluidity can be a result of many different factors, including the expression of certain biologically directed characteristics, hormonal influences, personal or spiritual exploration, living in different environments and interacting with different communities, and having significant sexual or romantic experiences.

Human sexuality is a complicated concept, and it can be difficult to apply simplistic ideas to try to define a person's sexuality or to put them in a box. Sometimes when we can't identify someone with one type of sexual preference, it can make us feel uncomfortable because we are unsure of how to interact with or talk to them. We may have questions about why someone can show this kind of sexual fluidity when we ourselves feel like it's "in our nature" to know our sexual orientation and have it be something that is fixed and unchangeable. Or perhaps we have our own thoughts about wanting to explore our sexuality in nontraditional ways, but we worry about what others might think of us or say about us behind our backs.

QUESTIONING YOUR SEXUALITY CAN HAPPEN AT ANY AGE.

Researchers have come to acknowledge that sexual orientation exists on a continuum. Some people talk about an exclusive attraction to the opposite sex, whereas others are exclusively attracted to the same sex, with others somewhere in between. Some people are mostly attracted to other individuals who also describe themselves as bisexual/being interested in both cisgender males and females, whereas others may more readily identify as being asexual and not generally attracted to people. Some might feel more comfortable with describing themselves as *pansexual*, or not limited in sexual attraction with regard to biological sex, gender, or gender identity.

People also define attraction in different ways and may feel that they are drawn to different people with regard to sexual, romantic, aesthetic, and emotional aspects of attraction. This is likely where terms like *demisexual* (people who only become attracted to others once they have formed an emotional bond), *sapiosexual* (people who require intellectual chemistry to become physically and sexually attracted to someone), and *skoliosexual* (people who are attracted to others who fall outside the typical gender binary) have been used to more accurately describe specific forms of sexual attraction.

It may be helpful to think about sexual orientation as going beyond language such as someone going through a "phase" or someone denying what should be natural. As we look at the world around us and get into conversations with people different from ourselves, we are likely to find that traditional labels for sexual desire don't capture the full spectrum of experiences people can have as they understand and

RESEARCHERS HAVE COME TO ACKNOWLEDGE THAT SEXUAL ORIENTATION EXISTS ON A CONTINUUM.

LET THEM KNOW THAT THEY SHOULD NOT FEEL PRESSURED TO DEFINE THEIR SEXUALITY WITH A LABEL, AND ENCOURAGE THEM TO TAKE AS MUCH TIME AS THEY NEED TO FIGURE OUT WHAT THIS ALL MEANS.

describe their sexual orientation to others.

Whether your teen is questioning their sexual orientation or struggling to relate to people whose sexual orientation differs from their own, it is important to give them the space to ask questions and find trusted people to discuss these issues with. If they're exploring their own sexuality, encourage them to try to separate their exploration and questioning from morality, or what they may have been taught about what is right and good. Remind them that their sexual exploration is normal, and there is no "wrong" sexual identity. More than anything, it is important that they feel they are being authentic to who they are and have the freedom to consider questions germane to their sexual orientation. Encourage them to think back on their relationships so far and people they've found attractive, without judgment, and see if any themes emerge. Let them know that they should not feel pressured to define their sexuality with a label, and encourage them to take as much time as they need to figure out what this all means. Max agrees with this—she says there is no deadline to figure all of this out, and it's true. Most of all, be there to hold them up when they feel alone, and let them know that no matter what they're experiencing in relation to their sexuality, they don't have to go through it alone. Help them to find nonjudgmental people who are good listeners to bounce ideas off of, and ask them to consider talking with a mental health professional for additional support and guidance.

never happen to someone in the queer community. This is no one's story but their own. I tried to backpedal with him and told him that I might actually not be bi, and he told me that he figured it would just be a phase. That was so invalidating to hear and really showed his true character. (Yes, I did keep going back to him. I know. Ugh, teenage "love." I am now much more aware of the respect I deserve and how I should be treated. But don't worry—it's gonna make one heck of an album.)

Eventually, I shared with most of my friends that I was bisexual. I told my best friend first and slowly shared the information with more and more people. Once I got comfortable with the information, I went on to tell my family and, ultimately, the internet.

TELLING THE FAMILY

I know I'm lucky in the fact that I never felt any fear around how my parents would respond to my coming out. I mostly didn't want to tell them because I didn't like talking about boys with my family, so it felt weird to say, "Oh, hey, I'm also attracted to girls." It just felt gross, which I think is something most teenagers would understand. You don't want to talk to your parents about anything related to attraction, sex, whatever—it's just not something you really want to bring up. But I also didn't want it to seem like this secretive thing.

Late in my freshman year, I kind of casually put it out there to my mom. I said, "I might like girls and guys; I don't know, blah, blah, blah." I was just kind of testing the waters, seeing if it would be an awkward conversation, because I hate awkward conversations. At the time, she asked me, "Have you ever kissed a girl?" I was like, "No, of course not." (Actually, I had, more than a few . . . but I didn't want to tell her that.) I never doubted for a second that she would be supportive, but that was kind of it—I brought it up that one time, and then we never discussed it again.

About a year later, during COVID-19 quarantine, I had *a lot of time* to think, like everyone else. (I think quarantine really was a sexual awakening for a lot of people—I know about twelve girls who came out during quarantine.) I had gotten a lot more comfortable with my sexuality and felt like my self-acceptance had grown so much. And I just thought, "You know, f*ck it. I am over this. I would rather just have everyone know. Judge me for what you want. I don't really care because I just want to be authentic to who I am—because what's the point if not? I could die at any moment." Which is kind of gruesome, but it's true.

I told my twin brother first, and he was super supportive and encouraging. And it ended up that he (he's straight) and I can talk about girls together, and I can bond with his friends over it. I think that's something that was unexpected—that you can share something you feel will be surprising or shocking to someone (or *not* surprising, in the case of my mom, lol . . .) and you think might push you apart, but instead, it brings you together. I know this isn't always the case and that families can be cruel and cold, or even worse, in response to someone coming out. But they can also be supportive and loving and encouraging.

Nicky said to me, "I want you to tell our parents. Be yourself. They will love you. I love you. It doesn't matter what people think of you anyway, but I am here for you. If you can tell them, tell them, but tell them when you're ready. But I want you to be able to live your full, authentic self."

I finally went to my mom and thought I was telling her for real for the first time. I said, "Mom, I'm bi." And she said, "Yeah, I know. You told me." And I said, "I thought you forgot. I thought it was just something we talked about once, and you probably thought it wasn't true." But she had already heard and accepted me . . . which is hilarious and amazing. My mom's the best.

"Sexuality is not like one size fits all. It's just like mental health; everyone, every experience, is different."

—J., California, sixteen

Then I wanted to get the whole family over with. I had my mom text my dad because I just felt like it would be an awkward conversation, and I wanted to avoid that. He said he loved me and nothing would ever change that. He made some jokes about the awkward-conversation comment, which was a perfect change in topic. He knew exactly what to say and has been very kind and accepting throughout the whole process.

I HOPE THAT'S WHAT WE'RE HEADING TOWARD, WHERE YOU DON'T HAVE TO COME OUT BECAUSE "DIFFERENT" HAS BECOME JUST NORMAL.

When I told my sisters, they were both so completely chill. I told my youngest sister, Coco, who was probably ten at the time, and she just said OK, as if it was nothing at all. I told her being bisexual meant that I liked boys and girls, and she just repeated *OK*. I think that's such a positive, telltale sign of how Generation Alpha is being raised—it's not even a thing you need to come out as anymore. I hope that's what we're heading toward, where you don't have to come out because "different" has become just normal.

At that point, it seemed like I might as well post something on social media because I just felt like I didn't want to have any secretive spaces. Honestly, the only person I was hiding it from was my principal, given what happened to my friend. But I decided to come out publicly anyway. I ended up posting something first on Instagram saying that I was bi, and the response was mostly positive—a lot of friends I hadn't talked to in forever reached out, saying congrats and good job. Of course, there were some "Ews" added in, but whatever—not everyone is going to accept you for who you are.

As for my school principal, it ended up that his son, who also went to my school, read about my coming out on *People* magazine's website, and he sent me a text saying, "Hey, so my dad saw the article on People.com and said he loves all people no matter who they love." Which I guess I had mixed feelings about. On the one hand, it was so comforting to hear, and I was really happy that I knew my spot at school was safe. On the other hand, because my friend at the same school had been unable to participate in activities she loved just because of her sexuality, I felt nervous and apologetic. I know there is something to be said about having the Dubrow last name when something like this happens. The school probably did not want negative press, but at the same time, I wasn't involved in any religious activities at the school that I could have been kicked out of (which is the kind of stuff my friend had been involved in).

As far as coming-out stories go, I know I'm super fortunate to have the support system I have. Even before I told anyone, I was comfortable enough in how I thought my family would respond to explore the feelings I was having—and that kind of knowing in your heart that you will be loved, no matter what, is probably the greatest gift parents can give their kids. Of course, you don't want to just assume your kid knows that you would be accepting of them no matter what, which is why it's important to say out loud that you are OK with whatever sexuality your child expresses. I don't think you could ever *overexpress* this to them.

A QUEER PATH ISN'T ALWAYS CLEAR

Even with a solid support system, you can find yourself struggling with self-acceptance and worry about fitting in with any kind of community. I know I feared that I wouldn't fit in with gay or bi people. I was worried that I dressed too feminine or that I just had a "straight" look, whatever that means. I realize this sounds so naive, but I really didn't know what it meant to be bisexual in real life; until I met Rachel, I didn't know any bisexual people (although I later found out she's a lesbian) personally, so any sort of image I had was created by movies or TV shows. And then, once I did meet girls who were bi or gay, I thought I wasn't pretty enough because they were all stunningly gorgeous.

DR. JUDY'S NOTES

GENDER IDENTITY

Gender identity is your own internal sense of yourself as male, female, a blend of both, or neither. It is how you perceive yourself and how you describe yourself to the world. Your gender identity can be the same or different from your biological sex that was assigned at birth. And unlike outward gender expression, your gender identity is not always visible to others.

For many people, gender identity aligns with their biological sex. These people usually define themselves as *cisgender*. But for others, it can be different. Some people describe themselves as *transgender*, which means that they feel their gender identity is different from the biological sex they were assigned at birth. And then there are some people who describe themselves as *gender binary* or *genderqueer*, which means that they don't define themselves as genders that fit into traditional

> **YOUR GENDER IDENTITY CAN BE THE SAME OR DIFFERENT FROM YOUR BIOLOGICAL SEX THAT WAS ASSIGNED AT BIRTH.**

ideas of man or woman. Still others might describe themselves as *agender* (when they don't define themselves with any gender) or *gender expansive* (a person who has a more flexible gender identity than what is associated with typical gender binary definitions).

When it comes to gender expression, some people may decide to express their gender outwardly, through behaviors, their voice, how they dress, or other character-istics associated with certain gender roles. And others may decide to go through a biological transformation so that their bodies and sexual organs match the gender identity they feel most comfortable with—which may not be the one they were assigned at birth. This is typically a very big decision and can take years to carry out from start to finish. Usually, this involves discussion with family members and loved ones, multiple consultations with doctors and coun-selors, and a lot of self-exploration in order to understand the pros and cons and risks and benefits of this decision.

Sexual orientation is separate from gender identity. For example, transgender people may be straight, les-bian, gay, bisexual, queer, pansexual, or asexual. And it can take a while to sort out what this means for the indi-vidual and those the person dates or relates to. It is not uncommon for these questions to arise in a person's mind during the teenage years. And this is all normal. Don't judge yourself for having these questions or being curious about what it means when someone identifies as different from you.

SEXUAL ORIENTATION IS SEPARATE FROM GENDER IDENTITY.

Whatever your own beliefs are and wherever you are in your own gender-identity exploration and determination, know that the use of pronouns is a great way to acknowledge your own and others' gender identity. Pronouns are one of the ways we identify ourselves, and referring to people by the same pronouns that they use for themselves is a way that you can show respect and acceptance to someone different from yourself. Similarly, communicating the pronouns you like to use (such as *he*, *she*, *they*) allows others to communi-cate with you in positive ways and affirm your gender identity.

This is helpful and important even if you feel that your gender identity lines up with traditional ideas (for example, that your biological sex, gender identity, and gender expression are the same). But respecting and using the pronouns that people use for themselves is especially helpful when someone describes themselves with a gender identity that is not conventional to your experience, because you are showing them that you care about them during a time when they are possibly being targeted by others for being different.

WHATEVER YOUR OWN BELIEFS ARE AND WHEREVER YOU ARE IN YOUR OWN GENDER-IDENTITY EXPLORATION AND DETERMINATION, KNOW THAT THE USE OF PRONOUNS IS A GREAT WAY TO ACKNOWLEDGE YOUR OWN AND OTHERS' GENDER IDENTITY.

Here's a great way to find out a person's pronouns. Start by giving your own, and then ask them what pronouns they use to describe themselves. And if you make a mistake and accidentally use the wrong pronoun, that's OK. Just apologize and move on. Most people understand that it can take a while to use pronouns that might not seem prototypical or traditional. The most important thing is that you're trying your best. And if you're curious about gender identity, don't be afraid to have these conversations with people different from you or open-minded adults who will be patient and explore these important concepts with you. Gender identity is a crucial part of our self-concept overall, and it's essential that you don't deny yourself the opportunity to understand this more clearly in yourself and others you care about.

"If my sexuality changes, that doesn't mean I was 'wrong' before or that I'm indecisive! I'm figuring it out!"

—S., New York, sixteen

I thought about all of this a lot, so much so that it made me not want to come out. I felt like people were going to have the same judgments as I did and say things like, "She's not pretty enough, she's not butch enough, she's not whatever enough"—or that they were going to think I was faking it or doing it to get attention. A lot of people I know have that same fear, that everyone's going to think they're making out with girls to get the boys' attention. But who cares, really, if that's what they think? Of course, you care early on because all you can think about is, "What is everyone going to think of me when I share this news?"

If you have a child or teen who is questioning, there's a good chance they're having these kinds of struggles, wondering how or where or if they will fit in. It's not easy because there's this period of time where everything is in your head, and you can't even figure out whom to talk to or how to sort through all the details or find answers. Do I ask the gay friend of my parents? Do I just google it? Do I seek out support on social media? (More on this in a bit.)

Here are some things that helped me start to feel OK just being who I am.

LETTING GO OF LABEL PRESSURE

I think there's so much pressure, whether it's imagined or real, to label yourself when you're coming out. But these labels are just boxes that are meant to make things easier for other people to understand or to judge, and they are confining and limiting. They're created by heteronormativity and just society in general, and they've been implanted in our minds so that we think we have to be one thing or another. The truth is that no one owes anyone else a label.

THE TRUTH IS THAT NO ONE OWES ANYONE ELSE A LABEL.

That doesn't mean giving yourself a label can't be helpful. It felt easier for me to come out as bisexual. It helped me explain myself to my extended family and allowed me to not keep it a secret anymore. Even if it would have felt more accurate to say, "I'm questioning my sexuality; I don't fit the mainstream mold, but I'm just not sure where I'll end up eventually," that would have just been super weird. No one would really get that, except for someone who was feeling the same way . . . and I don't think my grandma would be that person who feels the same way. And if she does, then we have a lot more to talk about, lol.

REALIZING THERE'S NO DEADLINE TO HAVE YOURSELF FIGURED OUT

At some point early on in exploring my sexuality, I was introduced to this girl who was in my grade who was bi. She was the first girl I met who was bi and single, and we started talking or snapchatting or whatever. It felt like my first chance to have something with a girl, even a relationship. Then, I ended up not liking her as more than a friend, and it got my head spinning about maybe not liking girls after all, when I thought I had already figured myself out, and what was I going to do now?!

It's a hard process when you're a teen (and I'm sure as an adult too, but probably for different reasons). So much of life at that time is about who you're dating, who you like, all of that kind of stuff. Then, you add these questions about yourself, and you feel overwhelmed by the need to have it all figured out. Yet there's no real rush or deadline.

TEEN TALK

"It's a spectrum. Sometimes people have to experiment to know what they like."

—T., Texas, nineteen

"I wish my parents understood that we can still have the same times we did two years ago—I am not some stranger; I am your kid."

—Z, California, sixteen

You have to go through trials and errors; you have to let yourself have experiences—for example, if you're like me, dating different people of different genders.

I think that's another gift parents can give their kids: time and space to explore who they're meant to be, even if that feels really tough to watch or if you, as a parent, feel an urgency to get it resolved yourself. Most parents would likely rather explain to other family members or their friends that their child is [fill in the blank sexual preference] once. No one wants to go back and say, "Oh yeah, well, she's not bisexual anymore; she's just gay." But you know what? None of that really matters if what you want is for your kid to be happy.

UNDERSTANDING THAT NOTHING IS PERMANENT

Another thing that helped me be able to come out as bisexual was realizing that I was allowed to change my mind. That's the beauty of sexuality—you can always change your mind if your preferences shift and find the person you love no matter who they are. We can always be learning about ourselves and changing, and expressing this as a reality can help educate others. I can be bisexual today, a lesbian tomorrow, and then decide I'm going to marry a man next week. And that's OK.

I am living proof that nothing has to be permanent in terms of sexuality. I started out considering myself bisexual (if I have to pick a label), but now I say that I'm a "bisexual-leaning lesbian." In some ways, the only reasons I like guys are (1) male validation and (2) daddy issues (I love my dad more than anything, but I do everything in my life for his approval). But you know, I'm still a work in progress. Anything can happen!

TO MY FELLOW QUESTIONING AND CURIOUS TEENS: FIGURING OUT WHO YOU WANT TO LOVE DOESN'T HAVE TO BE LONELY

Parents, most of this book is for you, but right now, I'd like to talk to your teens.

When you're trying to understand and explore your sexuality, it can feel like you're doing a lot of lonely work in your heart and head. But it doesn't have to be that way. I think it's really helpful to confide in someone you trust, whether that is an adult or a parent or a friend.

If it's an option, I would completely recommend talking to your parents and family. It's not as bad as you would think, if you think your parents will be accepting and understanding. If you're instead in a situation where your family is extremely unsupportive, and you would feel unsafe if you told them, maybe wait until you go to college or move out. You 100 percent should live your true happiness and your true life, but you have to make sure you're safe first. (If you are in this position, be sure to check the end of the book for resources that can help you.)

If your family is not an option, you can also consider talking to a teacher, coach, or theater director. I know a lot of my friends really trust their English teachers and have come out to them before anyone else. No matter who it is, you want it to be someone you trust, or if it's not someone you trust, maybe it's someone you don't even know who doesn't know you. You could try taking a writing class or improv class and telling complete strangers. That way, you could get it off your chest with a rehearsal of sorts, and you wouldn't have to endure any emotional response from anyone.

Another option is to find someone in the queer community to talk to. The queer community is so welcoming and ready to accept you with open arms; all my friends I know who are gay or bi or queer would be actually ecstatic to help someone. They are more likely to understand what you're feeling, and (a) they would not tell anybody, and (b) they have been there. Not only can they attest to it, but they can give you advice and tell you what they have been through.

The most important thing is to try to find an outlet for your curiosity, questions, and confusion. If you're a teenager, you already have so much going on, so much to do, and it's just generally a difficult time. If you can confide in at least one person, even just one person who will accept you and let you talk through your process, it will make such a big difference.

If you can't find anyone, you can connect with so many people on social media, on TikTok especially. You can look up LGBTQ+, WLW, or other terms you wonder about or might think you identify with. Once you land on those pages, you can rant and reach out in the comment sections and have people help you. They will give advice, and you can listen and connect. It's really amazing, and it's accessible to everyone. Of course, you can also search the internet for queer communities where you might be able to connect to a role model or just someone older than you who can offer guidance about your challenges.

And don't forget the option of therapy, which is such a good way to get support. If you are experiencing a lot of emotional challenges and difficulty in coming to terms with your sexuality, absolutely go see someone or find one of the phone- or text-based therapy options. If you are a parent and your child says they need to go to therapy, and you have the means to get them there, help them—and try to give them space to talk it through in therapy first if that's what they need; that is, don't force them to talk to you if they're not ready.

Ultimately, if you are the one trying to figure yourself out, you have to return to your own process of self-acceptance. For me, I relied on a lot of different outlets. I would type it out in my notes on my phone and sing a lot or write songs about my experience. You can journal, draw, dance, whatever your thing is—just find something to help you process your thoughts and feelings in a productive way.

DR. JUDY'S NOTES

DOES YOUR TEEN NEED PROFESSIONAL SUPPORT?

It is critical for parents (and treatment providers) to think about how to best support their teens who might be exploring their sexual orientation or gender identity. When you see this happening in your child, you may feel puzzled, worried, or even angry. All of these feelings are OK. Don't deny your own emotions; many parents have expectations or assumptions that don't rise to the surface of conscious thought most of the time. You may be worried that your teen's questioning or exploration is abnormal in some way or that perhaps somehow you are at fault. But none of this is true. It's very normal for teens to have questions about their sexuality and gender identity, especially during a time when, developmentally, they are forming their ideas about themselves, understanding who they are and how others see them, and actively working on building their self-esteem.

As a parent, you may have very fixed notions about what is "right" and "wrong" in terms of how people, and especially your children, should express their gender identity or sexual orientation. Try your best to put these ideas aside for the moment, or work out any difficult feelings with trusted friends and family members. Then, turn your focus to how

> **YOU MAY BE WORRIED THAT YOUR TEEN'S QUESTIONING OR EXPLORATION IS ABNORMAL IN SOME WAY OR THAT PERHAPS SOMEHOW YOU ARE AT FAULT. BUT NONE OF THIS IS TRUE.**

IT IS CRUCIAL THAT YOU TRY TO PUT YOUR OWN FEELINGS AND PRIOR BELIEFS ASIDE TO SUPPORT YOUR TEEN BECAUSE THE CONSEQUENCES OF NOT DOING SO CAN BE NOTHING SHORT OF DISASTROUS.

you can best support your child, and think about what will be the most helpful for them. Research shows that LGBTQ+ youth seriously contemplate suicide at almost three times the rate of heterosexual youth, and they are almost five times as likely to have attempted suicide compared with heterosexual youth. Importantly, LGBTQ+ youth who come from highly rejecting families are 8.5 times more likely to have attempted suicide compared with LGBTQ+ youth who reported no or low levels of family rejection. It is crucial that you try to put your own feelings and prior beliefs aside to support your teen because the consequences of not doing so can be nothing short of disastrous.

If your teen expresses gender-nonconforming ideas and/or does not describe themselves as straight in their sexual orientation, make sure they know that you are trying your best to understand their experience while not being able to know firsthand how they feel (unless your gender identity and/or sexual orientation also aligns with that of your teen). Think about what you say before you say it because verbal and nonverbal messages that reinforce the gender binary (gender as classified by only two forms, male and female) can be harmful for teens who are trying to explore these issues and already anticipate judgment and ridicule from others. Try to make sure your home environment feels safe for them, and if there are other family members who might have some ideas or judgments about such exploration, have conversations with them and educate them on how to give your teen some space as they try to figure things out. The Trevor Project, for example, offers a number of free, helpful resources for parents to support LGBTQ+ youth.

IF YOUR TEEN IS BEING BULLIED OR DISCRIMINATED AGAINST BY THEIR PEERS OR OTHER ADULTS, ASK HOW YOU CAN HELP AND IF THEY'D LIKE YOU TO INTERVENE.

If your teen is being bullied or discriminated against by their peers or other adults, ask how you can help and if they'd like you to intervene. Feel free to ask your teen nonjudgmental questions about how they are feeling, and ask them if they would like someone to talk to if you see them struggling emotionally with the exploration. Gender-nonconforming and sexually-nonconforming children are at higher risk for emotional stress, social withdrawal, anxiety, and depression, and if their exploration of gender and sexuality is causing them significant distress or affecting their ability to tend to their daily activities and responsibilities, encourage them to get professional help.

As a parent, you can start by interviewing mental health professionals regarding their experience with adolescents and stressors related to their gender and sexuality exploration. Ask them about their training, their experience, and the possible therapeutic approaches they might take with your teen to help them feel better. It's a good idea to interview a handful of therapists, narrow it down to your top three, and then give your teen some agency to choose the therapist they feel the most rapport and trust with. These are sensitive and deeply personal issues, and it is important to let your teen know that no matter what your own ideas and beliefs were at the outset, you love them unconditionally and will try your best to help them through the process.

I'm always saying to be your true self as long as you can be. But if you're in a situation where it's unsafe to come out or be who you want to be, who you *know* you are, then you might need to wait. That's a terrible situation, but you have to look out for your well-being and your safety before all else. This is true for adults and kids, and there are lots of available support options (see the Resources section at the end of the book).

If you have or know a child or teen who is questioning, please consider being the person who offers support. Maybe make it a point to be open about your acceptance of the queer community.

Even young people who you might think are supported and safe may be struggling with their own internal conflicts. I have plenty of friends who are gay or bi who have internalized homophobia, mostly because religion has taught them that it's wrong. I know a girl who would go to church every morning and pray that she wouldn't like girls. That's a lot of religious trauma, and it's a painful way to live.

I'm not saying that you want to go out of your way to bring it up with teens, because most teens will quite literally do anything possible to avoid awkward conversations with adults. But if you're the carpool mom or dad, the teacher, the coach, or whatever, and you get the chance to be that voice of support, take it!

THE FUTURE LOOKS BI

I hope that society gets to the point where kids really do learn that there isn't just one way to have a love story in your life. I think queer culture has done so much to revamp the rules around relationships and to show that humans can express and experience love in many different ways. It can be tough if you come from a place where there's just one narrative, the one-man-plus-one-woman narrative, to open your mind to all this newness. But it has changed and is constantly changing. More people are hearing the message that you don't have to live a life confined by certain expectations, and I feel lucky to be living at this time. I hope that if you love someone who has come out or is questioning, you can help them find the right resources and confide in the right people so that they can live their authentic self and be as happy as they can.

WHAT PARENTS SHOULD KNOW

Teaching your kids that the heteronormative story—that guys like girls, girls like guys, and that's it—isn't the only story can help them think about who they are in a way that's open and inclusive, whatever their sexuality or gender identity.

- A teen **exploring their sexuality** doesn't have to be experimenting with sex. Exploration is often first about sorting through feelings of attraction, thoughts, and related emotions.
- Give your kid **time and space** to explore who they're meant to be; this can be especially invaluable for a questioning teen. You can provide time and space while still offering your **support and acceptance**.
- If your teen needs help that you can't offer—and they probably will—the best thing you can do is help them **find the right support**. You can search together for local LGBTQ+ youth support groups or find a therapist who specializes in teen sexuality. If you stay connected to this part of the process, you will open the door to continued communication.

Being a teen in today's world is hard; being a teen who is questioning their sexuality can be even harder. Your love, support, and acceptance can change literally everything about their experience.

RESOURCES FOR TEENS WHO IDENTIFY AS LGBTQ+ (AND FOR PEOPLE WHO WANT TO UNDERSTAND MORE)

All teens need a positive social environment and supportive networks to thrive. However, LGBTQ+ teens may experience more difficulty feeling understood and connected compared to their peers who do not identify as LGBTQ+. Whether you are a parent to an LGBTQ+ teen, would like to help educate your teen on how to support LGBTQ+ teens in their social circle, or want to learn more about how you can support the LGBTQ+ individuals within your community, the following resources can be very informative and provide action steps on how to interact with LGBTQ+ individuals so that they feel validated, affirmed, and cared for:

Gay, Lesbian, and Straight Education Network (GLSEN)
Empowers teens to make change in their school and community
https://www.glsen.org/resources/student-and-gsa-resources

Gender and Sexualities Alliance (GSA) Network
Student-run organizations that unite LGBTQ+ and allied youth to make an impact around issues affecting their communities
http://www.gsanetwork.org/

It Gets Better Project
Uplifts, empowers, and connects LGBTQ+ youth around the world
https://itgetsbetter.org/

For additional resources, please see page 167.

ALL TEENS NEED A POSITIVE SOCIAL ENVIRONMENT AND SUPPORTIVE NETWORKS TO THRIVE.

hope that reading this book will help teens grow into self-sufficient, independent adults and set parents on a positive course for an open and honest relationship with their teens. It's not easy to be a teen or to parent one, but I truly think that focusing on communication, trust, and love can make it so much easier for everyone!

Max Dubrow

hope this book has offered some helpful guidance on how to best support your teen during a crucial time of physical, mental, emotional, and social development. More than anything, your teen will appreciate your effort to understand their unique experience and to give them support when they need it most. As much as they may push you away at times, know that deep down, they are likely searching for your approval and acceptance as they navigate this challenging time in their lives. Show them that you are open to learning from them while also offering valuable guidance from your own experiences. With some thoughtfulness and care, this can be one of the most wonderful periods of development in your relationship with one another. And as your teen develops more skill sets and resilience to face life, you can rest assured that you've given them all the tools they need to navigate their future with confidence.

Indy Ho

RESOURCES

TEEN MENTAL HEALTH

Mental Health Literacy
https://mentalhealthliteracy.org/

World Health Organization – Adolescent Mental Health
https://www.who.int/news-room/fact-sheets/detail/adolescent-mental
-health

National Alliance on Mental Illness – Teens & Young Adults
https://nami.org/Your-Journey/Teens-Young-Adults

HealthyChildren.org – Mental Health and Teens
https://healthychildren.org/English/ages-stages/teen/Pages/Mental
-Health-and-Teens-Watch-for-Danger-Signs.aspx

SELF-HARM OR SUICIDE

Teen Line
Teen to teen confidential helpline
1-800-TLC-TEEN (call or text "teen" to 839863)

Your Life Your Voice
For preteens, teens, and young adults
1-800-448-3000 (call, text, chat)

Crisis Text Line
Text "youth" to 741741 to reach a trained counselor

The Trevor Lifeline
For LGBTQ+ teens
1-866-488-7386 (call, chat, or text "start" to 678-678)

National Suicide Prevention Lifeline
1-800-273-TALK (call or chat)

National Alliance on Mental Illness
1-800-950-NAMI (call or text "NAMI" to 741741 if in crisis)

Mental Health America
Referrals for local mental health professionals
https://mhanational.org/finding-help

Psychology Today
Referrals for local mental health professionals
https://www.psychologytoday.com/us/therapists

CYBERBULLYING

StopBullying.gov
https://www.stopbullying.gov/

ConnectSafely – The Parent's Guide to Cyberbullying
https://www.connectsafely.org/wp-content/uploads/cyberbullying
_guide.pdf

CallerSmart – What Is Cyberbullying and How to Stop It
https://www.callersmart.com/guides/49/cyberbullying-what-is
-cyberbullying-and-how-to-stop-it

Internet Safety 101
https://internetsafety101.org/

Delete Cyberbullying
https://www.endcyberbullying.net/

Common Sense Media – Cyberbullying, Haters, and Trolls
https://www.commonsensemedia.org/cyberbullying

Stomp Out Bullying
https://www.stompoutbullying.org/

RELATIONSHIP ABUSE

National Domestic Violence Hotline
thehotline.org
1-800-799-SAFE (call, chat, text)

Love Is Respect
National teen dating abuse helpline
https://www.loveisrespect.org/
1-866-331-9474 (call, chat, text)

National Sexual Violence Resource Center – Teen Dating Violence Prevention Resources
https://www.nsvrc.org/blogs/teen-dating-violence-prevention
-resources-2021-update

Teen Dating Violence
https://www.teendvmonth.org/resources/

LGBTQ+

Gay, Lesbian, and Straight Education Network (GLSEN)
Empowers teens to make change in their school and community
https://www.glsen.org/resources/student-and-gsa-resources

Gender and Sexualities Alliance (GSA) Network
Student-run organizations that unite LGBTQ+ and allied youth to make an impact around issues affecting their communities
https://gsanetwork.org/

It Gets Better Project
Uplifts, empowers, and connects LGBTQ+ youth around the world
https://itgetsbetter.org/

The Trevor Project
Crisis intervention and suicide prevention for LGBTQ+ teens and young adults (including 24/7 hotline)
https://www.thetrevorproject.org/

PFLAG
Information about peer support and education in local communities
https://pflag.org/

Family Acceptance Project
A research, intervention, education, and policy initiative to prevent health and mental health risks for LGBTQ+ youth
https://familyproject.sfsu.edu/

CDC – Parents' Influence on the Health of Lesbian, Gay, and Bisexual Teens: What Parents and Families Should Know
Information on how parents can promote positive health outcomes for their LGBTQ+ teen
https://www.cdc.gov/healthyyouth/protective/pdf/parents_influence_lgb.pdf

INTRODUCTION BY DR. JUDY

AAP News. "Children's Hospitals Admissions for Suicidal Thoughts, Actions Double During Past Decade." May 04, 2017. https://www.aappublications.org /news/2017/05/04/PASSuicide050417.

Agoston, Anna M., and Karen D. Rudolph. "Interactive Contributions of Cumulative Peer Stress and Executive Function Deficits to Depression in Early Adolescence." *Journal of Early Adolescence* 36, no. 8 (2016): 1070-1094.

Bethune, Sophie. "Teen Stress Rivals That of Adults." *Monitor on Psychology* 45, no. 4 (April 2014): 20. https://www.apa.org/monitor/2014/04/teen-stress.

Flannery, Mary Ellen. "The Epidemic of Anxiety Among Today's Students." NEA News. Updated March 2019. https://www.nea.org/advocating-for-change/new-from-nea /epidemic-anxiety-among-todays-students.

Geiger, A. W., and Leslie Davis. "A Growing Number of American Teenagers— Particularly Girls—Are Facing Depression." July 12, 2019. https://www.pewresearch .org/fact-tank/2019/07/12/a-growing-number-of-american-teenagers-particularly -girls-are-facing-depression/.

Menasce Horowitz, Juliana, and Nikki Graf. "Most U.S. Teens See Anxiety and Depression as a Major Problem Among Their Peers." Pew Research Center. February 20, 2019. https://www.pewresearch.org/social-trends/2019/02/20/most-u-s-teens-see -anxiety-and-depression-as-a-major-problem-among-their-peers/.

National Institute of Mental Health. "Anxiety in Teens Is Rising—What's Going On?" Accessed July 1, 2021. https://www.healthychildren.org/English/health-issues /conditions/emotional-problems/Pages/Anxiety-Disorders.aspx.

CHAPTER 1

Dishion, T. J., and R. J. McMahon. "Parental Monitoring and the Prevention of Child and Adolescent Problem Behavior: A Conceptual and Empirical Foundation." *Clinical Child and Family Psychology Review* 1, no. 1 (1998): 61–75.

CHAPTER 2

Centers for Disease Control and Prevention. "Adolescent Health." Accessed August 9, 2021. https://www.cdc.gov/nchs/fastats/adolescent-health.htm.

Centers for Disease Control and Prevention. "Data and Statistics on Children's Mental Health." Accessed July 1, 2021. https://www.cdc.gov/childrensmentalhealth/data.html.

Centers for Disease Control and Prevention. "Sexual Identity, Sex of Sexual Contacts, and Health-Risk Behaviors Among Students in Grades 9-12: Youth Risk Behavior Surveillance." Atlanta, GA: U.S. Department of Health and Human Services.

Children's Hospital of Philadelphia. "Suicide and Self-Harm." Accessed August 9, 2021. https://violence.chop.edu/types-violence-involving-youth/suicide-and-self-harm.

Curtin, Sally C., and Melonie Heron. "Death Rates Due to Suicide and Homicide Among Persons Aged 10–24: United States, 2000–2017." NCHS Data Brief, no 352. October 2019. https://www.cdc.gov/nchs/products/databriefs/db352.htm.

Geiger and Davis, "Growing Number of American Teenagers."

Grover, Rachel L., Golda S. Ginsburg, and Nick Ialongo. "Childhood Predictors of Anxiety Symptoms: A Longitudinal Study." *Child Psychiatry and Human Development* 36, no. 2 (2005): 133–153.

Ho, Judy. *Stop Self-Sabotage: Six Steps to Unlock Your True Motivation, Harness Your Willpower, and Get Out of Your Own Way.* New York: HarperCollins, 2019.

Menasce Horowitz and Graf, "Most U.S. Teens."

CHAPTER 3

Casale, Silvia, Laura Rugai, and Giulia Fioravanti. "Exploring the Role of Positive Metacognitions in Explaining the Association Between the Fear of Missing Out and Social Media Addiction." *Addictive Behavior* 85 (October 2018): 83–87. https://doi.org/10.1016/j.addbeh.2018.05.020.

Clayton, Russell B., Glenn Leshner, and Anthony Almond. "The Extended iSelf: The Impact of iPhone Separation on Cognition, Emotion, and Physiology." *Journal of Computer-Mediated Communication* 20, no. 2 (March 1, 2015): 119–135. https://doi.org/10.1111/jcc4.12109.

Lenhart, Amanda. "Teens, Social Media & Technology Overview 2015." Pew Research Center. April 9, 2015. https://www.pewresearch.org/internet/2015/04/09/teens-social-media-technology-2015/.

National Crime Prevention Council. "Cyberbullying: What Is It?" Accessed August 9, 2021. https://www.ncpc.org/wp-content/uploads/2017/11/NCPC_Cyberbullying-WhatIsIt.pdf.

Primack, Brian A., and César G. Escobar-Viera. "Social Media as It Interfaces with Psychosocial Development and Mental Illness in Transitional Age Youth." *Child and Adolescent Psychiatric Clinics of North America* 26, no. 2 (April 2017): 217–233.

Rideout, Victoria. "The Common Sense Census: Media Use by Tweens and Teens." 2015. https://www.commonsensemedia.org/research/the-common-sense-census-media-use-by-tweens-and-teens.

CHAPTER 4

Bessiere, Katie, Sarah Pressman, Sara Kiesler, and Robert Kraut. "Effects of Internet Use on Health and Depression: A Longitudinal Study." *Journal of Medical Internet Research* 12, no. 1 (2010): e6.

Broadbent, Stefana. "Approaches to Personal Communication." In *Digital Anthropology*, edited by Heather A. Horst and Daniel Miller, 127–145. New York: Berg, 2012.

Centers for Disease Control and Prevention. "Youth Risk Behavior Surveillance—United States, 2019." *Morbidity and Mortality Weekly Report* 69, no. 1 (August 21, 2020): 1–83.

Green, Melanie C., Jessica Hilken, Hayley Friedman, Karly Grossman, Josephine Gasiewskj, Rob Adler, and John Sabini. "Communication via Instant Messenger: Short- and Long-Term Effects." *Journal of Applied Social Psychology* 35, no. 3 (March 2005): 445–462.

James, Carrie, Katie Davis, Linda Charmaraman, Sara Konrath, Petr Slovak, Emily Weinstein, and Lana Yarosh. "Digital Life and Youth Well-Being, Social Connectedness, Empathy, and Narcissism." *Pediatrics* 140 (November 2017): S71–S75.

Kang, Seok. "Disembodiment in Online Social Interaction: Impact of Online Chat on Social Support and Psychosocial Well-Being." *CyberPsychology and Behavior* 10, no. 3 (June 2007): 475–477.

LaRose, Robert, Matthew S. Eastin, and Jennifer Gregg. "Reformulating the Internet Paradox: Social Cognitive Explanations of Internet Use and Depression." *Journal of Online Behavior* 1, no. 2 (January 2001).

Lenhart, "Teens, Social Media & Technology."

Lenhart, Amanda, Aaron Smith, Monica Anderson, Maeve Duggan, and Andrew Perrin. "Teens, Technology and Friendships." Pew Research Center. August 6, 2015. https://www.pewresearch.org/internet/wp-content/uploads/sites/9/2015/08/Teens-and-Friendships-FINAL2.pdf.

Lomanowska, Anna M., and Matthieu J. Guitton. "Online Intimacy and Well-Being in the Digital Age." *Internet Interventions* 4, no. 2 (May 2016): 138–144.

Moody, Eric J. "Internet Use and Its Relationship to Loneliness." *CyberPsychology and Behavior* 4, no. 3 (June 2001): 393–401.

Rideout, Victoria. "The Common Sense Census: Media Use by Tweens and Teens."

Steiner, Riley J., Ganna Sheremenko, Catherine Lesesne, Patricia J. Dittus, Renee E. Sieving, and Kathleen A. Ethier. "Adolescent Connectedness and Adult Health Outcomes." *Pediatrics* 144, no. 1 (July 2019): e20183766. https://pediatrics.aappublications.org/content/pediatrics/144/1/e20183766.full.pdf.

CHAPTER 5

Ainsworth, Mary D. S., and Silvia M. Bell. "Attachment, Exploration, and Separation: Illustrated by the Behavior of One-Year-Olds in a Strange Situation." *Child Development* 41, no. 1 (1970): 49–67.

BabySparks. "Infant-Parent Attachment: The Four Types and Why They Matter." June18,2019.https://babysparks.com/2019/06/18/infant-parent-attachment-the-four-types-why-they-matter/.

Bessiere, Pressman, Kiesler, and Kraut, "Effects of Internet Use."

Bowlby, John. *Attachment and Loss*. New York: Basic Books, 1969.

Broadbent, "Approaches to Personal Communication."

Centers for Disease Control and Prevention, "Youth Risk Behavior Surveillance."

Centers for Disease Control and Prevention. "Over Half of U.S. Teens Have Had Sexual Intercourse by Age 18, New Report Shows." June 22, 2017. https://www.cdc.gov/nchs/pressroom/nchs_press_releases/2017/201706_NSFG.htm.

Divecha, Diana. "How to Cultivate a Secure Attachment with Your Child." February 3, 2017. https://greatergood.berkeley.edu/article/item/how_to_cultivate_a_secure_attachment_with_your_child.

Green, Hilken, Friedman, Grossman, Gasiewskj, Adler, and Sabini, "Communication via Instant Messenger."

James, Davis, Charmaraman, Konrath, Slovak, Weinstein, and Yarosh, "Digital Life and Youth Well-Being."

Kang, "Disembodiment in Online Social Interaction."

LaRose, Eastin, and Gregg, "Reformulating the Internet Paradox."

Lenhart, "Teens, Social Media & Technology."

Lenhart, Amanda, Monica Anderson, and Aaron Smith. "Basics of Teen Romantic Relationships." October 1, 2015. https://www.pewresearch.org/internet/2015/10/01/basics-of-teen-romantic-relationships/.

Lenhart, Smith, Anderson, Duggan, and Perrin, "Teens, Technology and Friendships."

Lomanowska and Guitton. "Online Intimacy and Well-Being."

Main, Mary, and Judith Solomon. "Procedures for Identifying Infants as Disorganized/Disoriented During the Ainsworth Strange Situation." In *Attachment in the Preschool Years*, edited by Mark T. Greenberg, Dante Cicchetti, and E. Mark Cummings, 121–160. Chicago: University of Chicago Press, 1990.

Moody, "Internet Use."

Rideout, "Common Sense Census."

Sroufe, L. Alan. "Attachment and Development: A Prospective, Longitudinal Study from Birth to Adulthood." *Attachment & Human Development* 7, no. 4 (2005): 349–367. https://doi.org/10.1080/14616730500365928.

Steiner, Sheremenko, Lesesne, Dittus, Sieving, and Ethier, "Adolescent Connectedness."

CHAPTER 6

Savin-Williams, Ritch C. "Sexual Orientation: Categories or Continuum? Commentary on Bailey et al. (2016)." *Psychological Science in the Public Interest* 17, no. 2 (April 25, 2016): 37–44. https://doi.org/10.1177/1529100616637618.

Stanford Vaden Health Services. "Sexual Fluidity." Accessed June 22, 2021. https://vaden.stanford.edu/health-resources/lgbtqia-health/sexual-fluidity.

MAX DUBROW is the host of the hit podcast *I'll Give It to You Straightish*. She covers a variety of topics on her show, ranging from life as a bisexual Jewish teenager at a strictly Catholic high school to influencers, social media, mental health, and more. Known for her appearances on Bravo's *Real Housewives of Orange County*, Max is no stranger to the public eye and uses her platform to shed light on the very real pressures today's teens are facing.

DR. JUDY HO is a triple board certified and licensed clinical and forensic neuropsychologist, a tenured associate professor at Pepperdine University, and a published author. Her most recent book, *Stop Self-Sabotage*, was published by HarperCollins and has been translated into seven languages. Dr. Judy maintains a private practice in Manhattan Beach, California, where she specializes in comprehensive neuropsychological assessments and expert-witness work. She regularly appears as an expert psychologist on television, podcasts, and radio; contributes to other media including print and electronic periodicals; and often speaks at national and local conferences and workshops for organizations and schools. Her treatment approaches integrate the scientific principles of cognitive behavioral therapy, acceptance and commitment therapy, and dialectical behavioral therapy.

Dr. Judy received her bachelor's degrees in psychology and business administration from UC Berkeley, and her master's and doctorate from SDSU/UCSD Joint Doctoral Program in Clinical Psychology. She completed a National Institute of Mental Health–sponsored fellowship at UCLA's Semel Institute.